WHAT PEOPLE ARE SAYING ABOUT
WEAPONS OF MASS DECEPTION

"I could not be more proud of my husband for showing true vulnerability when writing *Weapons of Mass Deception*. He went through a really dark season that our entire family experienced, but I can say today that our home is filled with peace and joy. These weapons are real. And whether you are reading this for yourself or for your loved one, it's worth it to take a courageous leap of faith to find your true purpose. You can have the life that you never imagined was possible. Thank you for fighting for yourself and your girls, Babe. Continue Mission."

—JESSICA JONES

"I was present with Adam on the frontlines as the words of this book were being forged in the crucible of his own journey. I was present as a brother to help him through dismantling his own weapons of mass deception. That is why I can stand here with great confidence to say this book is a library-essential for any high-performing leader who is ready for life to be more than just increasing stress and anxiety. If you're truly ready for answers and the work required, you are holding the guide that will get you to places that have only existed in your daydreams. Until now."

—DAVID FARWELL, CEO, Catalyst, and Consultant, The Resurgence Network

"When I hired Adam as my coach, I had no idea how profoundly he would impact my life. His methods, which are laid out in this book, provided the new paradigms I needed to finish my book and pursue more purposefully my life's mission. Through storytelling, spiritual insight, and military organization, Adam brings a powerful punch that you will feel from the very first chapter. Read it. Study it. Devour it."

—PHIL MERSHON, author of *Unforgettable: the Art and Science of Creating Memorable Experiences*, Director of Experience at Social Media Examiner

"With over 40 years of experience working in the mental health profession, first as a clinician and then later as the chief of several mental health clinics, I'm inspired by Adam's message. It's needed more than ever. There are many books on leadership and team building, but Adam brings it to a deeper level. He examines the innermost character of the leader needed to ignite a team and family."

—ALAN JONES, Lieutenant Colonel, U.S. Army (Retired); Medical Service Corps, Fellow of the American College of Healthcare Executives (FACHE)

"My family attended an event where we heard Adam speak about these weapons, and we were blown away. Thank you, Adam, for standing up for freedom. Your faith and wisdom are helping so many with the mental struggles they face!"

—LYNDSIE HINCH, Owner, Makeup Design Studio

"In today's society, people are so caught up in the 'here and now,' they are oblivious to the deceptions that have permeated their lives. We need more focus, attention, and direction on what really matters, and my friend, Adam Jones, is equipping you with the tools you need to truly succeed. I've known Adam for over 10 years, and the transformation I've seen in his own life speaks volumes regarding what he is honestly and openly communicating to you. Read and hear what he has to say—it is profoundly deep, yet remarkably simple."

—EDWIN "SCOTT" CHAPIN, Chief Warrant Officer 4, U.S. Army; Mentor, Educator, and Aviator

"*Weapons of Mass Deception* will empower you to stand strong against the onslaught, recognize tactics used against you, and counter maneuver effectively. One typically considers adding a book to your library. This one would be better conceptualized as adding weapons to your arsenal."

—DAVID MCCRERY, Retired Law Enforcement Officer, SWAT Team Operative, Sniper, Hostage Negotiator, and Police Academy Instructor

"Adam has a mission in this book. It is to reveal the lies regarding how we value ourselves based solely on our position and purpose. What will we do when those things change? How will we handle it? I believe his message is overdue and critical to change the culture of veterans and mission-minded leaders. I believe *Weapons of Mass Deception* is needed and long overdue."

—GREG MOORE, U.S. Army Veteran

"For two years, I've been personally coached and trained by Adam. He is an effective leader who knows his purpose and his identity. People need to hear this message of freedom."

—DALE TIKKANEN, VP, Motus Financial, Inc.

"I have no doubt this message of restoration from the weapons of mass deception that Adam discusses will resonate and transform lives."

—DAN BEAVER, Cybersecurity Consultant

Copyright © 2023 by Adam F. Jones

Published by Kudu Publishing

All rights reserved. No portion of this book may be reproduced, stored in a retrieval system, or transmitted in any form or by any means—electronic, mechanical, photocopy, recording, scanning, or other—except for brief quotations in critical reviews or articles, without prior written permission of the author.

Scripture quotations marked NIV are taken from the Holy Bible, New International Version®, NIV®. Copyright © 1973, 1978, 1984, 2011 by Biblica, Inc.™ Used by permission of Zondervan. All rights reserved worldwide. www.zondervan.com. The "NIV" and "New International Version" are trademarks registered in the United States Patent and Trademark Office by Biblica, Inc.™

For foreign and subsidiary rights, contact the author.

Cover design by: Simon Parry
Cover photo by: Julie Watkins @juliewatkinsphotos

ISBN: 978-1-959095-32-3   1 2 3 4 5 6 7 8 9 10

Printed in the United States of America

WEAPONS OF MASS DECEPTION

Detect and Defeat the Four Weapons
Destroying Your Peace, Purpose, and Power

ADAM F. JONES

Dedication
For my girls.
You are more than I could ever dream.
When the world tells you who to be,
remember who you already are.
Live with **GRIT**.
G*ive Grace.* **R***espect Life.* **I***nvite*
Others. **T***ake Action.*
And . . .
you will move mountains.

CONTENTS

Foreword xi

Introduction 17

PART I. **DEFINE THE WEAPON** 25

CHAPTER 1. Life-Changing Lessons 27

CHAPTER 2. The Bottom Line 33

CHAPTER 3. The Breaking Point 41

CHAPTER 4. Wandering in the Wilderness 57

CHAPTER 5. The Weapon That Wages War 67

CHAPTER 6. The Heart, the Home, and the Headquarters 75

PART II. **DETECT THE DECEPTION** 87

CHAPTER 7. Drift Happens 89

CHAPTER 8. Weight of the World 97

CHAPTER 9. You're Leaving Again? 107

CHAPTER 10. "Only a Truck Driver" 117

CHAPTER 11. Who Have I Become? 129

CHAPTER 12. Battle Damage Assessment 141

PART III. **DISMANTLE THE WEAPON** 149

CHAPTER 13. Trust Your Instruments 151

CHAPTER 14. Break the Kill Chain 177

CHAPTER 15. Seeing the Shift................................ 195

CHAPTER 16. Prioritizing Our People 199

CHAPTER 17. Owning Our Story 209

CHAPTER 18. Breaking the Ceiling 223

CHAPTER 19. My New Declaration 227

PART IV. **DEPLOY THE COUNTERATTACK** 237

CHAPTER 20. Deploy the Tactics........................... 239

CHAPTER 21. Blue Sky...................................... 263

About the Author 273

Acknowledgments.. 275

FOREWORD

Adam Jones amazes me!

As a transformational and executive leadership coach for the past forty years, having had the privilege of addressing and coaching the likes of presidents, royal families, and business executives, I find Adam to be a truly transformational leader.

Nothing speaks louder than one's own life, and this book is a bold step in sharing his own story of radical transformation in hopes that it may stir, encourage, and spur you on in your own journey forward.

This book is not just a good idea; it is truly a testimony of his own personal journey—a journey where he has conquered the weapons of mass deception in his own heart and is now passionate about seeing that success transpire in others' lives!

When I first met Adam on a five-day leadership challenge that I was hosting, I was immediately drawn to him. It was clear to me that he was a young man with a lot of promise. He had energy, focus, determination, drive, and a NEED to succeed. He was also a young man who was clearly facing, as he calls it, attacks from the weapons of mass deception. Weapons that were spreading into all areas of his life.

This type of young leader is not uncommon to find among emerging leaders as life is, after all, a journey of growth. We are all challenged with our own weapons of mass deception. It is unfortunate, though, that many compromise or stall on their growth journey and end up suffering major casualties in their home and families and their own perception of self as a result. These weapons of mass deception have taken out too many good men and women, and they need to be dismantled!

According to Business Group On Health approximately 800,000 people commit suicide a year globally.[1] Suicide is the fifteenth leading cause of death globally for all age groups, the second for young people aged 15 to 29, and the fifth for those aged 30 to 49. This, simply said, is a tragedy! Mental health is a serious and very real problem among emerging leaders. One of the triggers of mental health is long-term stress. *When a leader does not deal with the stresses that come from extreme hustle and resorts to "the grind" in order to gain status and influence, this unsustainable stress becomes suppressed in the heart and unfortunately finds itself working out into one's relationships, marriage, family, and home.* This often inflicts great loss in all of the above areas, simply because they had such a NEED for success without first knowing *who* they are.

Our sociocultural influences often determine how we approach life, what values we put on, and how we see success. For example, if you were in the military for any amount of time (which both Adam and I were), then you will most likely be driven by performance and

---

[1] "Suicide: An Increasing Concern for Global Employers," *Suicide: An Increasing Concern for Global Employers | Business Group on Health*, 9 Jan. 2020, https://www.businessgrouphealth.org/resources/suicide-an-increasing-concern-for-global-employers.

the need to achieve and succeed which, in turn, may lead you to seek affirmation from others as the source for your personal identity and worth. This is, unfortunately, very unhealthy. This is also how I found Adam!

When you can only see as far as your past, your present and future can both be underwhelming and overwhelming. When you view life through the lens of someone searching, not sure if you belong and constantly looking for a "well done" as opposed to the secure belonging that comes from being truly loved and accepted for WHO you are and not just what you've accomplished, life can seem like an unending obstacle course you're ultimately due to fail at. The pursuit to measure up, often initiated in your own mind but commonly perpetuated through life's broken and imperfect relationships, can lead you on the merry-go-round of desire: the desire to be seen, the desire to be truly accepted, and the desire to make a difference.

Adam's transformation began when he recognized his need to connect through genuine relationships and even other father figures. Not a literal or biological father but rather a relational figure or community. Someone who leads with authority but who isn't looking to advance his own agenda. Someone who could see in Adam what he wasn't even able to see in himself. He became curious, open, and determined to invest in challenges, programs, and relationships that would challenge, connect, and empower him toward the future he could only dream of having. This is where we met.

His curiosity had him asking the right questions.

His openness connected him to valuable relationships where giving and receiving was both mutual and beneficial.

His determination pushed him forward when he was tempted to settle, think smaller, or give up.

His transformation today is evident. His growth journey is still being written because he hasn't stopped growing.

From an orphan mentality to the security of knowing he belongs.

From a child to a son.

From one who sees through the broken lens of "Am I enough?" to one who sees through the grace-filled lens of "I'm already loved."

From one paralyzed and minimized by weapons of mass deception that were working against him to one running and overcoming through the constant pursuit of growth and significance but, this time, coming from a place of security in knowing *who* he is as well as what he has to give. This transformation hasn't just grown him personally but has resulted in a compulsion to give, see others empowered, and help them turn their weapons of mass deception into a testimony they will share to empower others. From one transformation to another!

I'm excited for you to become the hero of your story, just as Adam has become in his! This book is filled with simple and strategic understanding that will have you dismantling the weapons of mass deception in your own life that have kept you from moving forward as the transformational leader you were designed to be—full of peace, power, and purpose!

My desire is that you would find your own story of belonging as Adam has found his. That your breakthroughs would lead you to harmony in your home, positive growth in your relationships, and a wealth that is found in more than simple monetary success. That peace would be your constant companion, purpose would be the driving force pulling you forward, and power would mark your growth journey as a transformational leader, pulling others from their point of "stuckness" to greatness.

This book is a must-read for all who believe that they are called to be a leader—who believe that they are destined to transcend the average in life. I love the verbiage that Adam uses to bring clarity to that which seeks to undermine this destiny journey of yours. Read; then, find within you the tenacity to commit to the process of change that will truly bring you to living a sustainable, holistically successful life.

This book is a transformational read written by a transformed transformational leader!

—Dr. Israel McGuicken

INTRODUCTION

As an aspiring army pilot, during initial entry rotary wing training (aka flight school), I learned something that I will never forget. Two chapters can make or break a pilot. Two chapters in a five hundred-plus page operator's manual. The 5s and 9s. Chapter 5: Aircraft Limitations and Chapter 9: Aircraft Emergency Procedures. Two chapters that must not only be read but remembered—over fifty pages that require every line to be rote memorized and recalled daily because they are deemed that important.

At any point in the day, my instructor pilot could ask me to recite how I would respond to an aircraft emergency—and I had to get it right. I had to respond perfectly. Word for word. Without hesitation. Nothing could be missed. Every word mattered. Why? Because everyone on the aircraft—including me—could *die* if I didn't know them.

Now, let's back up a few years. When I started learning to fly at twelve years old, I also had to be aware of my aircraft limitations and emergency procedures. I had to know where to find information and how I would initially respond, but I didn't have to memorize every word and number. Why the difference? I'm not a rocket scientist, but I think it has to do with the mission. The army was training me to become a professional pilot. The work I would do would be directly tied to a mission and the preservation of the lives of many men and women. There was no room for error. No time to pull out a checklist to see what steps I should take.

Just curious. What kind of training do you remember getting for life? Think about that for a moment. What if we viewed life as a training ground? I'm not talking about preparing for some natural disaster. I'm talking about training our minds to respond to the challenges of life, override false beliefs and destructive thoughts, and respond to the chaos of parenting. How are you training to lead your family today?

> **WHILE HIGH-PERFORMING LEADERS HAVE HONED THEIR SKILLS AT PUTTING OUT FIRES IN THEIR WORKPLACE, THEY REALLY DON'T HAVE A CLUE HOW TO RESPOND TO A FAMILY CRISIS, A CRYING BABY, OR AN AGGRAVATED SPOUSE.**

I've found that most high-performing leaders, while they've honed their skills at putting out fires in their workplace, they really don't have a clue how to respond to a family crisis, a crying baby, or an aggravated spouse. (I didn't.) We live in a time where everyone is told to do more, hustle more, and just keep going regardless of the warning signs. Therefore, many men and women ignore or don't even know what their limitations are or how to monitor them. They just keep going, suppressing everything. (At least, that's what I did.)

If you're a man, do you wear a "Mask of Masculinity"[2] as Lewis Howes calls it? If you're a woman, does what Dr. Marybeth Crane calls "Superwoman Syndrome"[3] plague you? Both men and women hide behind their success. We find a way to win in our careers, often at the expense of losing in our homes. How many marriages fail because of tension caused by a lack or an excess of communication, resulting in misunderstanding? It might be helpful for us to learn some 5s and 9s for life, don't you think?

When things fall apart—and they will—we almost always revert back to our training. In fact, my first engine failure (yep, it actually happened) occurred when I was in flight school. It was on my first solo flight; I didn't have to fly with an instructor pilot. I was flying with a fellow student, and instead of heading back to base, we were headed toward the ground. Luckily, we had an open field off our nose, so we executed the emergency procedure and lived to fight another day. I'm really glad they made me memorize those procedures. I'm grateful I had the tools to avert disaster.

Language is a tool. However, it can also be a barrier. Basically, without the proper language, we miss out on what we're trying to say as well as what we're trying to understand. The purpose of this book is to equip you with tools—the language to communicate and the perception to understand—and to invite you on a journey of expansion. In the military, we would go about sharing this information through

---

2 Lewis Howes, *The Mask of Masculinity: How Men Can Embrace Vulnerability, Create Strong Relationships, and Live Their Fullest Lives* (Emmaus, PA: Rodale Books, 2017).
3 Dr. Marybeth Crane, *Drop The S; Recovering From Superwoman Syndrome* (Stonebrook Publishing, 2021).

a SITREP—a Situation Report. In our case, the SITREP would look like this:

SITUATION REPORT (SITREP)

Weapon of Mass Deception:

Any act of hidden malicious intent that exploits another person's insecurities or motives in order to deter, delay, dissuade, or destroy a multitude of people.

Target: High-Performance Leaders

The primary target for this weapon is the high-performance leader. Their drive, determination, and desires put them at a high risk for exploitation.

High-performance leaders have been trained to restrain their emotions and suppress their feelings in order to protect others and accomplish their goals. Shaped by a mission-focused culture. Formed in the crucible of challenge. A new battle is waging in their hearts and spreading through their homes. For years, they were immersed in a self-sustaining system of processes, procedures, and protocols that provided the structure they needed to connect to purpose and power.

Without those systems—they are lost.

Threat: Weapons of Mass Deception

Weapons of Mass Deception have found their target in the heart of mission-minded leaders. Often, exploiting a vulnerability in leaders' ambitions, these weapons focus on bringing destruction and chaos to their lives. Mobilized by a persistent but predictable plan of attack and concealed in thought patterns, their greatest strength is secrecy.

Exploiting a leader's motives to serve. Seducing him with a promise of impact. Luring her down a path of destruction. Overloading leaders with a burden of perfection. Their purpose is clear: complete annihilation.

Four primary weapons of mass deception have been identified. Each weapon follows an attack structure of systematically spreading from the heart to the home and finally into the headquarters (i.e., the workplace). This attack structure is what makes weapons of mass deception so deadly.

Cleverly concealed as a solution to a leader's search for significance, afterward, they perpetuate aggression, addiction, and emptiness. We cannot allow the unseen nature of the threat to allow us to underestimate its destructive capability. If this threat is ignored, many other people will pay the price.

Action: Operation Restoration

The threat's strength lies in its secrecy. Our greatest response to defeat this menace is to reveal its covert nature and launch a decisive counterattack with Operation Restoration. This response not only removes the effects of the threat but empowers high-performing leaders and their families to rise up with strength.

Operation Restoration involves four simple phases:
> Define the Weapon.
> Detect the Deception.
> Dismantle the Weapon.
> Deploy the Counterattack.

I have two objectives for us through this book: I want to *expose* a weapon and *equip* you to find freedom. I'll do this by sharing personal stories as well as those of colleagues whose names have been changed for the sake of their privacy, baring the cracks in my armor, and presenting principles and lessons I've learned on my journey that have absolutely changed my life.

> **I HAVE TWO OBJECTIVES FOR US THROUGH THIS BOOK: I WANT TO EXPOSE A WEAPON AND EQUIP YOU TO FIND FREEDOM.**

Considering the well-known sentiments of an unknown author: "The only thing necessary for the triumph of evil is for good men to do nothing," it is critical we acknowledge the presence of evil. Evil exists, and it is determined to destroy those who stand for good.

My language in this book may seem either too strong or too soft, depending on your perspective. What I'd recommend is an open mind and a willingness to change and grow. Every one of us is at a different stage of our life's journey. Some will resonate with *Weapons of Mass Deception*'s easygoing and relaxed language. Others need to hear the intensity.

I don't know where you are. You might be one fight away from losing your marriage or moments away from alienating your kids. Maybe you're contemplating whether or not you should stay in the fight. You might feel it's hopeless—that for every win, there is another defeat lurking around the corner. Regardless, I believe in Operation Restoration down to my core. I believe in you and your family. And

I believe that you are on your way to progressing from a maxed-out leader to a transformational leader.

By utilizing your current skills, implementing the processes in this handbook, and executing Operation Restoration, we can see freedom prevail once more in the hearts, homes, and headquarters of high-performing men and women worldwide.

PHASE 1
DEFINE THE WEAPON

"The empires of the future are empires of the mind."
—Winston Churchill[4]

---

4 "Churchill, Culture, and Soft Power," edited by Alasdair Donaldson, *British Council*, Nov. 2015, https://www.britishcouncil.org/research-policy-insight/insight-articles/churchill-culture-and-soft-power.

CHAPTER 1
LIFE-CHANGING LESSONS

Nothing is more painful than seeing your family experience destruction from a life that you've created. No one knows this reality better than maxed-out, high-functioning leaders. These men and women realize they have nothing left to give. They've given everything, and it's still not enough. It's a reality that can be seen during various stages of life but most often during a stage of transition.

Seeing the pain in my wife's eyes taught me many things about the complexities of weapons of mass deception, but three core lessons guide me today.

AMBITION

The first lesson became so significant that it inspired a new core value that I live by: *Ambition must be aligned to and provide availability for the accomplishment of your assignment.* If your ambition fills up your schedule and removes your ability to say yes to the greater assignments in your life, then it's time for a realignment of your priorities. For me, after learning this lesson, I realized that my assignments are clarified through my relationship with God. Clear connections to actions that God has set up for me always come with a greater level of impact and transformation. Things such as family, relationships, and places of impact that I'm called to are assignments that I do my best to remain focused on and available for today.

To help reinforce this, I've adopted that new core value that I mentioned: availability. Think about it. The greatest leader lives a life of mission but also maintains a level of availability. Weapons of mass deception love to exploit your ambition in order to remove your ability to fulfill your assignments. They love to weigh you down and distract you from the greater purpose of your life. Don't let them.

WEAPONS OF MASS DECEPTION LOVE TO EXPLOIT YOUR AMBITION IN ORDER TO REMOVE YOUR ABILITY TO FULFILL YOUR ASSIGNMENTS. THEY LOVE TO WEIGH YOU DOWN AND DISTRACT YOU FROM THE GREATER PURPOSE OF YOUR LIFE. DON'T LET THEM.

INFLUENCE

Second, *extended service that abdicates our areas of influence is selfish.* When we abandon our territory and shirk our responsibilities of leadership for those who need us most, we are acting selfishly. Trying to grow a larger company while not serving those we've already been entrusted with. Spreading ourselves thin by joining a bunch of organizations to inflate our egos. Sadly, I see this all the time with goal-oriented men and women. Their blind obsession with serving and making an impact in the world ruins their ability to expand their influence over those closest to them.

Leadership trainer Dr. Sam Chand explains that a legacy is not about *what* we leave behind but *who* we leave behind.[5] Whom are you leaving behind and equipping to carry your influence? This is core to understanding our second lesson.

In the Netflix series, *The Last Kingdom*, King Alfred of Wexford is chosen to rule and expand his kingdom.[6] Imagine if King Alfred just decided to leave Wexford with no plans for his return. What would happen if he just decided to start volunteering his time to help an organization in another kingdom while his citizens waited for him to return?

Noble service or not, it is unnecessary. He has a responsibility to those he is already leading, right? Over time, they will wonder where their king is. Did he forget about them? As months go on and seasons change, they become worried as they see the kingdom of Wexford deteriorate. They eagerly await King Alfred's return, but he's going around to all these villages in other kingdoms, seeing where he can help out. He feels more appreciated by them, so he continues his escapade while his people are in pain. They need him to resolve issues, but he's off furthering some other cause, abdicating his current place of leadership. How pissed would his citizens be? How abandoned would they feel?

Do you see how crazy that is? One of the greatest acts of service for a king is to actually serve those people who are in his territory. One of the greatest acts of service for us is to serve the people who have

---

5 Sam Chand, "Leave a Legacy," *Sam Chand*, 2 June 2020, https://www.samchand.com/blog/leave-a-legacy.
6 Stephen Butchard, *The Last Kingdom*, Netflix, 10 Oct. 2015.

already chosen to be led by us. Your wife chose you, right? Your husband chose you. So why are we avoiding them?

If we are constantly leaving to go help others, abdicating our responsibilities as a parent and a spouse, it's probably time for a realignment, like I mentioned in the first lesson. I totally get it. This was me in every shape and form. That is why I'm stressing this lesson so strongly right now. Your family needs you to lead.

> **WEAPONS OF MASS DECEPTION LOVE TO DRAW MEN AND WOMEN AWAY FROM THEIR ASSIGNMENTS, MAKING THEM THINK THE NOBLEST THING THEY CAN DO IS SACRIFICE THEIR ROLE WITH THEIR FAMILY IN ORDER TO HELP OTHERS.**

In a mission-driven culture, where we emphasize service above self, it is easy to think "self" includes our investments in our family or other pieces of our territory. We think that it's selfless to sacrifice time with our family. But if we're willing to be real with each other, we both know it is often easier to volunteer for the next opportunity or to stay late for work than it is to stay boxed up in a home full of stress. I'm all for selfless service, but I also want us to see that one of our greatest opportunities to serve is experienced by engaging as a parent, a spouse, and a leader.

Weapons of mass deception love to draw men and women away from their assignments, making them think the noblest thing they can do is sacrifice their role with their family in order to help others.

COMMUNICATION

Third, *intentional conversations create transformational change.* We cannot downplay the power of words. The Bible says that God spoke and created life. In fact, I'm convinced that the only thing that will ever fulfill your desire to live a mission that matters is to align your words to the life you want to live. In my progression from hurting to healed, angry to peaceful, and empty to revived, many conversations had to take place when I took off the uniform.

The same will most likely be required of you.

Some conversations brought awareness, teaching me that the pain I was feeling wasn't an isolated event but, instead, a systematic shared problem among most high-achieving leaders. Some conversations brought alignment, helping me create order within the deeper plans for my life and family and realizing that results follow alignment. Other conversations brought activation, providing me with new skills and insights to unlock solutions and mobilize into mission. Regardless, I'm sure of one thing. The right conversation can change a destiny.

> I'M SURE OF ONE THING. THE RIGHT CONVERSATION CAN CHANGE A DESTINY.

In the next chapter, I invite you into some of the pivotal conversations that changed my life. My hope is that by hearing my progression—and even seeing the destruction—you will begin to see the signs in your own life and join me in bringing transformation to your heart, home, and headquarters.

CHAPTER 2
THE BOTTOM LINE

I remember one day thinking to myself, *Why do I feel so empty? Who am I? Does everyone see through tired eyes like mine? Is it normal to feel so depleted for so long?* Despite all of those thoughts, I thought if I just kept pushing forward, if I just did a little more, it would get better. What I didn't realize was that, for once in my life, *doing* more was not going to help me *become* more.

Today, I wonder if it's possible that we've become so accustomed to suffering for the sake of others' gain that we have neglected to enjoy our own freedom. Is it possible that as we have been hardened by and against the challenges in the world, we've allowed them to also harden our hearts? A battle-hardened mindset might have shifted into a hardened heart. We might see others with annoyance and disdain. We might be fighting to find peace, but it seems pointless because the only way we are finding it is with pills or a bottle.

What happens when you realize that what you thought you'd been *suppressing* has only been *spreading*. Will you just fake it for the sake of your family, or will you be real?

When your toddler is screaming for her third popsicle, your exhausted spouse is rushing around in the kitchen preparing meals for tomorrow, dishes are piling up in the sink, your dogs are barking to go outside, your job feels meaningless, and your newborn is screaming because the milk isn't warm enough, so you have to wait for it to heat up even more, how do you respond?

What do we do when we feel like we're going to lose it?

> ONE MORE DEPLOYMENT. ONE MORE DEGREE. ONE MORE RANK. ONE MORE PROMOTION. . . . WHEN WILL IT EVER BE ENOUGH? WHEN WILL WE BELIEVE THAT WE ARE ENOUGH?

One more deployment. One more degree. One more rank. One more promotion. Maybe that's what we are missing, right? Just one more enticing carrot dangled in front of us with the promise of reward. When will it ever be enough? When will we believe that we are enough?

I don't think we'll ever answer that through the voice of someone else—from an outside source. We have to hear it from within. I had to hear it from my Creator. The chances of that happening with such a barrage of loud voices telling me to hurry, max out, and hustle were slim until I learned to shut them up. I'm going to show you how to do the same thing.

BOTTOM LINE UP FRONT (BLUF)

Let's get right to the point. As a speaker and tactician, I'm not really a fluff guy, so I don't want to waste time. This book is going to be intense.

That's just my personality. I'm the guy who has to slow down and ask myself, *What does fun look like, and how do I have fun with family?* Thank God for my wife because she keeps me on track.

If you or someone you know is about to crash, you don't have time to waste. In the fast-paced culture of the military, when people get wordy trying to explain something, they are often quickly interrupted and reminded to just give the Bottom Line Up Front (BLUF). (It's so effective it's been integrated into the corporate world and marketplace too.) If a leader has questions after hearing the BLUF statement, they'll ask them.

So here's the BLUF that I want you to understand immediately. The majority of high-performance leaders are targeted by at least one of four weapons of mass deception:

1) One weapon weighs us down by a pressure to get it right, to do it perfectly, and to find our value in our latest measurement.
2) One weapon causes us to drift from those who need us most based on our diluted focus and overly ambitious pursuit of impact.
3) Another steals our joy by causing us to feel like no matter what we do, it's never good enough and that we have never been enough.
4) The last weapon diminishes our power based on our reliance on prior labels and current titles.

When all of these weapons are mobilized against us, the effects can actually be deadly. I'm not exaggerating. This is one reason we're seeing depression, divorce, and death from suicide at rates higher than ever before.

Systematic thoughts and beliefs are driving our behaviors and leading us to destruction, and we can't even see them. What I found was that as *I* tried to suppress the stress and tension, *my wife* could feel it. In other words, it confirmed what I'd already suspected: what we suppress in our hearts spreads into our homes. We aren't fooling anyone. We might not notice it right away. We think if we just hold it all in, everyone else will be okay. We will be the only ones to suffer. However, this only works for so long.

Since these weapons will target anyone with ambition, every high-impact man or woman, whether young or old, is likely feeling the effects of their destruction, and without training to detect the threat, it will only get worse.

If you've experienced a strong streak of success in your past, I'm sure you've learned that despite all the achievements, it's never enough, and it will never be enough. If you don't believe me, just listen to some of the *Leadership Accelerator* podcast episodes in which we've interviewed high-performing leaders, and you'll hear that deception doesn't discriminate.[7] These weapons target firefighters, SWAT officers, detectives, sailors, airmen, fathers, mothers, businesspeople, husbands, wives, engineers, owner-operators, ministers, and people from all walks of life who are determined to change the world.

As a former Army National Guard Black Hawk helicopter pilot and captain, when I stepped out of the service, the destruction from all four of these weapons became evident in my life. I didn't have the language to recognize it for what it was or communicate it then, but the pain was real. And the worst part was that they weren't just hurting me but everyone around me.

I remember one day looking into the eyes of my wife and seeing a dull, tired look of disappointment staring back at me after I had let her down again. That caused me to wake up. What have you seen with your spouse, kids, or friends that just felt like a dagger to the heart?

---

7 "Continue the Mission Podcast," *Buzzsprout*, https://continuethemissionpodcast.buzzsprout.com/.

I've particularly noticed that when someone dedicates their life to the service of others, whether as a military member, first responder, or other public servant, they are even more vulnerable to these weapons. They experience pain most people will never know, and they've been trained to suppress their stress. They have become proficient at enduring the suffering. Their mind reinforces an automation where they downplay their feelings with no intention of changing. Only when we can *shift focus* and clearly see those who need us most will we see the freedom we are searching for.

I knew how to put on the mask of masculinity.[8]

I knew how to hide.

But when I saw the pain in my wife's eyes, when I thought of the future of my relationship with my firstborn daughter disintegrating, I knew it was time to change. Just like in the cockpit, I had to acknowledge my limits and use my emergency procedures. For the first two years after stepping out of the service, it was a struggle. Whether you are a veteran or not, we all have experienced massive transitions since the pandemic hit. It's crazy how the timing worked out, but only two months before COVID-19 shut down the world, I attended my final formation.

As I'll explain, it wasn't long before I found myself experiencing new feelings of loneliness and resentment.

Emptiness began to fill my heart.

I didn't know how to be present.

I couldn't understand how to move forward. I just felt trapped in transition.

---

[8] Lewis Howes, *The Mask of Masculinity: How Men Can Embrace Vulnerability, Create Strong Relationships, and Live Their Fullest Lives* (Emmaus, PA: Rodale Books, 2017).

> **WHAT I WAS SUPPRESSING IN MY HEART WAS SPREADING INTO MY HOME. THE MORE THAT I IGNORED THE WAR THAT WAS WAGING INSIDE MY HEART, THE WORSE IT GOT FOR EVERYONE ELSE.**

I didn't realize that each of the four weapons of mass deception was targeting not only my *heart* but my *home*. What I was suppressing in my heart was spreading into my home. The more that I ignored the war that was waging inside my heart, the worse it got for everyone else. I couldn't hide it any longer; I had to acknowledge a crash was coming. I remember thinking:

I'm drifting.
I'm maxed out.
I have no idea what to do now.

Something powerful happens when we surrender to a greater power, recognize that we don't have all the answers, and admit that we need some help. For me, my relationship with God was magnified during this time. When I said, *I have no idea what I'm doing. You take the controls, God. I'm done trying to lead my life since it's clearly not working.* That's when I began to develop the necessary tactics to not only detect these weapons but to disarm them from the inside out.

I'm not saying we are the only cause of everyone's stress and tension in our families; I'm saying we are either adding to it or taking it away. Leadership expert Dr. John C. Maxwell taught me that people are either adding to or subtracting from their relationships.[9] The same thing goes for you. Are you adding to the stress or taking it

---
9 John C. Maxwell, *21 Irrefutable Laws of Leadership* (Nashville, TN: Thomas Nelson, 2004).

away? Are you giving power to your family and friends, or are you taking it from them?

My hope is that when I share with you some of the patterns in my life, they will help you clearly see situations in yours with a new perspective. That you'll receive the tools to *define, detect, dismantle, and deploy* a solution for the very weapons that once caused you to suffer. That you will be better equipped to restore the heart of your home and bring the transformation that is needed during this time of your life.

There's no guarantee, but there's hope:
> Your heart will be revived and your marriage restored.
> Your relationships, both with your children and friends, will be strengthened.
> You'll see lives transformed because you showed up with clarity.
> And you will finally unlock the power in your presence like never before.

We can only give what we have:
> I can give peace because I have peace.
> I can give joy because I have joy.
> I can give confidence because I have confidence.
> That which I have, I can give.

And, I can guide you to experience that same transformation if you are willing to do the work. You'll begin to see clearly your limits and the emergency procedures that you need to implement as you follow this simple four-step framework to upgrade your confidence, connection, and clarity.

Today is the greatest day to begin. Let your best days be your next days, be a hero in your home, become the most attractive and magnetic person your spouse has ever met, and get ready to reach greater levels of influence. *Weapons of Mass Deception* won't just motivate you. It will *activate* you.

CHAPTER 3

THE BREAKING POINT

The sound of a text alert on my phone captured my focus. Glancing away from my computer for a moment, I looked down and saw a notification that my wife had sent me a text:

I'm just not happy. I do everything around here. I don't want you to defend yourself right now. I just want you to listen to how I feel. I don't feel loved by you anymore. I don't feel appreciated. It's like you take me for granted.

How's that for exposing the cracks in my armor and bringing awareness to the destruction through one conversation? I'm not going to hold back the scars of my past for the sake of my pride or ego. I hope you will have the courage to do the same. Your family is counting on it.

I knew she was right. It was hard to read, but when I finally grasped the reality of the message after staring at it for ten minutes, I realized, *This is one of those texts I'll never forget. It's time to either put up or shut up.*

> I'M NOT GOING TO HOLD BACK THE SCARS OF MY PAST FOR THE SAKE OF MY PRIDE OR EGO. I HOPE YOU WILL HAVE THE COURAGE TO DO THE SAME. YOUR FAMILY IS COUNTING ON IT.

The hardest part was that I didn't know how to fix it. My schedule was full, and my eyes were cloudy. It's hard to explain if this hasn't happened to you, but I literally felt like I had been looking through a foggy lens for months. It was like there was a film over my eyes. I had no clue how to be "more present," but it was obvious I needed to figure it out.

This was the warning call. This was the moment when the robot in the movie *Lost in Space* announced, "Danger, Will Robinson, danger."[10] I can imagine further explanation: *You are overloaded, drifting, and about to crash.*

Unfortunately, the crash was already happening, and I didn't know my emergency procedures. In fact, I was ignoring my growth as a husband entirely. I thought I could just check the boxes: I'm married, we love each other, good to go. But this text reminded me that marriage is work. Relationships take focus.

There was, however, a fragment of hope that maybe I could fix this. What a lie that is, by the way. How would I fix it? I'm the one who caused it. I needed something greater than me. My heart was hardened and guarded. I didn't need a quick fix. I needed a transformation. I needed a heart transplant.

---

10 Gene Bleile, "Danger, Will Robinson, Danger!" *Cape Gazette*, 22 July 2021, https://www.capegazette.com/article/danger-will-robinson-danger/223921.

Quick scripture reference: in Exodus in the Bible, we hear about Pharaoh hardening his heart to the people of God. I needed the opposite of that. I knew that I wasn't that fun to be around because I couldn't get out of my own head. I knew I wasn't compassionate or kind because I was always so serious. I didn't know how to be spontaneous and joyful. But if Pharaoh could harden his heart, I wondered if God would soften mine. What would the world look like if we had leaders with thick skin but soft hearts? Men and women who were moved with compassion—yet steadfast with conviction? I wanted to find out.

I had seen plenty of indicators along the trail that pointed to my depression and anger, but I ignored them. Eventually, my outbursts and feelings of emptiness built up to the point where I knew something was off, but I didn't know why. (Quick disclaimer: I never hurt anyone physically or anything like that. My anger would just be expressed through shutting down or a sharp comment.) I didn't have a traumatic experience from my time in the service. This was something else. Something much more common.

If you can relate to how I was feeling, just know that your transformation can come if you take it seriously. Chances are, your wife, husband, kids, friends, or whoever else is being affected by your decisions hasn't expressed to you the severity of the pain they feel right now, but I'm hopeful that through my story, you'll see it.

If you are in a time of *transition*, I think this next illustration might help you.

When studying the patterns of the four weapons, I noticed that they were planted in my heart years before I left the service. However, when I made my exit, I was exposed to their effects like never before. Here's a quick visual of how I see this in my mind. In the movie *Avengers:*

Infinity War, there is a powerful and all-consuming force field that protects the country of Wakanda.[11] This fictional country, located in East Africa, is home to the superhero Black Panther and becomes the final fight scene where warriors are taking their last stand to stay alive and preserve life on earth.

There is a scene where the force field is fully operational and protecting the citizens of the country effectively, but, eventually, small gaps begin to form. A swarm of enemies infiltrates the country of Wakanda, wreaking havoc and destruction by exploiting small vulnerabilities within the structure of the protective barrier. Think of this as being protected by a structure where you are comfortable.

If you were a military member, maybe this was the service. If you were a first responder, this could have been your department. You get the picture. But one thing is clear: when you stepped out of the comfort of your former structure, when you left that protection, you were exposed, and the damage from each weapon—whether it started while you were in or after you got out—became much more evident.

I want to be clear about this. I believe that for most people, the damage is happening while you're in, but once you leave that "force field," you are vulnerable to greater destruction than ever before. Just because you're protected, it doesn't mean you can't get attacked.

Some enemies will break through the barrier, but the community will protect you.

Some destructive thoughts will influence your mind, but the community can help detect them by pointing out the changes in your behavior and often bring you back into alignment.

---

11 Anthony Russo and Joe Russo, *Avengers: Infinity War* (April 28, 2013; Los Angeles: Marvel Studios), Dolby theater.

However, once you step out of the structure . . . it's like you've walked out from under the barrier shield, and you are fully exposed to the threat.

Before we can go forward, I need to take you back. It's time to rewind this story to show you a few moments when the destruction from each weapon of mass deception was evident, yet I still kept the blinders on, pressing forward in ignorance.

BEFORE WE CAN GO FORWARD, I NEED TO TAKE YOU BACK.

FATHER'S DAY POSER

"No Daddy!" my one-and-a-half-year-old daughter complained. "I want Momma."

"Addy, it's Father's Day. Can't you be nice to your dad?" my wife suggested.

"No! I don't want Dada."

"It's okay, Jess," I said, "I'm fine." Inside, I was feeling rejected and annoyed. *I work so hard to provide for this family. But it's never enough.*

This was my second Father's Day. It wasn't really going as I would have expected. Addy's rejection cut deep. I had left my career as an Army captain and Black Hawk pilot, so she could have me around more. For what? This?

Ironically, that day, I was wearing an OD (olive drab) green shirt with black letters that said GIRL DAD across the chest. Poser. *My own daughter doesn't want to be with me. No one gets me. I just want to be alone. Life was easier when I was in the military. At least then I would have an excuse to leave.*

I snuck off to find another beer to drown my thoughts. Tears fell down my face as I faded away from the barbecue. I'd been holding these back for months. This wasn't the first time my daughter had rejected me, but it was the worst it had ever hurt. It must have been the heightened expectations of Father's Day. While most fathers were being celebrated, I was just being tolerated.

A few moments later, we were in the car. Jess sat in the driver's seat, looked over at me, and saw it. The pain that I couldn't hold back. The empty stare with sunglasses over my eyes to hide the truth. But another tear fell onto my girl dad T-shirt. She saw it roll down my cheek. I didn't say a word. I just tried to hold it back. She looked at me. I was about six IPAs deep, my newly formed gut stretching the shirt. Everything was just falling apart. My body, my mind, my family . . . all headed in the wrong direction.

"Are you alright, Babe?" Jess asked.

No response.

"She doesn't mean it. You know she loves you, right?"

"Yep."

"Addy, tell Daddy you're sorry for how you treated him today. That wasn't nice."

No response.

The car began to back out of the driveway.

"Adam, is everything okay?" Jess asked.

I paused. Then I gave in, "No, it's not." I said, admitting defeat. "I'm not happy. Addy never wants me. I have no idea who I am. I just feel . . . empty."

"I'm sorry. Is it something I did? Are you not happy with us?"

"Jess, no. I don't know." Slowly, I began to try to find the words to describe how I felt, but I couldn't. I didn't know how to talk about it.

Then I remembered another guy, a guy we watched in a TV series.[12] He was going through some heavy depression after his career fell apart. He was married. Financially successful. But, empty. Like me.

"Jess, remember Rome from that show we watch? I feel like him. I need you to take this really serious because I'm telling you I feel like him, and I don't know what to do."

Right there, my progression toward a life of joy and freedom began. That is when my journey toward happiness officially started. I didn't know how to say what I was feeling, but I had an example I could point to. That was all I needed. An example. And that's what I hope to give you through this book: real language and real examples that you can point to and learn from. If that happens, I will have accomplished my intent. If that happens, your life will change forever.

I continued, "I'm so . . . angry lately. I feel so tired. I don't know what happened. [Cue the evidence of a weapon of mass deception.] I don't know anyone since we moved [more about that later], and I can't seem to get anything right."

Look, I'm not some social media influencer trying to show you how messed up my life was in order for you to follow me. I'm telling you this, so you'll understand you're not alone—and most importantly, so you can see your best days can be your next days. It's not over yet.

I mean, check this out: in the Army, I never even deployed. Like I said earlier, it's not that I had a traumatic experience overseas that caused this to show up. After nine years of service and three scheduled deployments that were canceled, I never experienced combat. Which, let me just say, really messed with me after I got out. I felt like I never really "served." I hated that question from civilians: "Did you

---

12 D. J. Nash, *A Million Little Things* (September 26, 2018; Burbank, CA: ABC Signature and Kapital Entertainment), Television.

go overseas?" I would have to say, "Nope. I stayed in the US the entire time." But in the back of my mind, I would think, *Nope. Did you? So, why are you asking?* (I'm just being honest!)

WEAPONS OF MASS DECEPTION ARE NOT JUST BRINGING DAMAGE TO OUR LIVES BASED ON WHAT WE'VE DONE. SOMETIMES, THEY WREAK HAVOC BECAUSE OF WHAT WE NEVER GOT TO DO.

Weapons of mass deception are not just bringing damage to our lives based on what we've done. Sometimes, they wreak havoc because of what we *never* got to do. I know plenty of great military men and women who are filled with shame for things *they were never chosen* to experience. They enlisted prepared to give all, but their country never called on them to make that sacrifice. While our country might have been at war, some (in their own words) "never fought." Some drove trucks. Others worked as communications specialists, hospital corpsmen, or electronics technicians. Some never shot a round overseas, and some didn't leave the wire (didn't leave base because they didn't receive a mission that required them to leave base). It's similar to having been part of a state championship team—as second or third string. Or, in some people's words—a "benchwarmer."

Trust me; nothing we do—or don't do—will ever be enough. Regardless of a high-performing leader's situation or realm of influence, that's exactly the type of belief that takes root in a heart and attracts the weapon in the first place. Weapons of mass deception grab you during times of shame and regret, whether those feelings are earned or not. I feel that God wants me to share some of my moments with you in order to help you process what's going on in your life. So I'm just going to put it all out there. You are not alone.

It wasn't just the lack of structure from the military that caused this for me. It was the loss of identity, the new location, the lack of community, misplaced expectations, and . . . I think you're getting it now—weapons of mass deception.

THE FLOOD

"This week has been ridiculous. I'm just glad we finally finished unpacking all those boxes. You set up the utilities, right? When did they say recycling comes?" Jess asked.

"Yep, utilities are set. I think they said they come every other Tuesday. I know; this week has been exhausting." My thoughts drifted to a project I was working on. *Man, that was fire. Can't wait for that episode to come out. I feel like podcasts are really going to be my sweet spot.*

"Did you get our washer hooked up?" Jess asked.

"What?"

"Did you hook up the washing machine like I asked?"

"Oh, yeah, good to go. I had to move some things around, but we are all set. Just threw a load in." I continued to think, *The only thing is that I really need to organize my framework to connect. . . .*

"How did the teachers say Addy did at school?" (For any young people reading this, infant daycare is called school.)

"Great. They said she ate all her lunch and was playing well with the other kids too."

"Awesome!" Jess exclaimed as she looked over at our daughter, "Good job, Addy girl. Do you want a chocolate pretzel?" (Our go-to treat.)

"Hey, how did your podcast interview go today?" Jess asked as she walked to the pantry to grab a chocolate pretzel. I thought she would never ask.

Bursting out in excitement, I said, "It was incredible! I talked about...."

Jess interrupted, "Is it raining outside...?"

"No... why would it be raining?" Wondering why she felt that was the right time to ask about the weather, I went on explaining how the interview went, "... how to leverage your lens based on your experience and...."

Jess blurted, "... then what's going on with our ceiling?"

"Huh, I don't know." *Can I get a word out please...?* "I don't see anything," I said as I glanced up. "What are you talking about.... Woah! What is that?" I trembled, noticing a dark spot forming above my head... consistently spreading further across the ceiling.

"Is our roof leaking?" she asked as water began falling from above.

"Maybe a pipe broke?"

I ran to grab something to catch the water. Finding a cooking pot, I dropped it on the floor. Glaring up, I saw the recessed can light dripping water. I frantically searched for the next container as Jess began to move the TV.

"Oh my God, wait!" I fumed as I realized what had happened. "Just stay down here, and find another pot for the water."

Stumbling up the stairs, I ran to the laundry room and found the source of the leak. Already noticing the soaked carpet through my socks, I smashed the power button on the washing machine and watched as the hose completed draining out any remaining water from the wash cycle.

"What's going on? Did you forget to do something when you set up the washer today?" Jess yelled upstairs.

Ignoring my wife, I ran to grab bath towels. *I can't believe this. I'm such a freaking idiot!*

"Adam, what happened?"

"Momma, I need my chocolate pretzel!" Addy complained.

"Hang on, I'm fixing it!" I yelled downstairs.

"It's getting worse."

"Woof, Woof." Reese, one of our family dogs, demanded as she glared at me with impatience.

"Mom. Chocolate," Addy began to whine.

"I need more towels. The washer is leaking! I forgot to put the hose back," I admitted.

I felt ridiculed by that voice inside. The snide, condescending voice of the weapon of mass deception hidden deep in my heart and mind. I just wanted a win. I was convinced our ceiling was destroyed. A successful day of business couldn't mask the deeper accusation pumping through my veins—that I couldn't even install a washer without messing it up.

And it's not that I didn't know how. It's that I skipped steps. I made a habit of filling every free minute of my day and corner of my mind with trying to be productive. Rushing through the day, trying to cram as much as I could into my schedule with no room to breathe. Never really completing the task at hand before moving on to the next one. Before one task was over, I was already thinking of the next. As a pilot, this is the kind of stuff that gets you killed.

> I MADE A HABIT OF FILLING EVERY FREE MINUTE OF MY DAY AND CORNER OF MY MIND WITH TRYING TO BE PRODUCTIVE. RUSHING THROUGH THE DAY.... NEVER REALLY COMPLETING THE TASK AT HAND BEFORE MOVING ON TO THE NEXT ONE. BEFORE ONE TASK WAS OVER, I WAS ALREADY THINKING OF THE NEXT. AS A PILOT, THIS IS THE KIND OF STUFF THAT GETS YOU KILLED.

Jess knew that I knew better. I just didn't care enough to finish the work around the house. She knew the podcast was more important to me than the priorities at home.

YOU PUT THE GROCERIES AWAY, RIGHT?

Two weeks had gone by since the flood.

The weight of the pressure of living in this new world at the height of the pandemic continued to grow. In the past four months, everything had changed. All that I saw as my normal had shifted. I was in a new home in a new state, doing a new job at a new business, and I hadn't worn my uniform since earlier that year. I had noticed how easily irritated and short I had been with those closest to me. I felt totally isolated and to be honest, kind of lost, but I told myself, *I gotta keep pushing because I know my life was meant for more than this.* I'd had some rough meetings that day. Nothing seemed to go right, but with only twenty minutes before the girls got home, I was going to clean up around the house. Maybe at least I could do that right.

Twenty minutes later, the front door opened, and the dogs rushed to greet the girls.

"Hey."

"Hey, Babe."

"Have a good day?"

"Yep, not bad. A few rough meetings," I replied, "just finished cleaning up around the house."

"Cool, thanks. I just need to get changed real quick, and then I'll start working on dinner so we. . . ." Jess paused as she noticed the kitchen countertop. Brown paper bags lined up next to each other. Unopened and full of perishable food.

"Wait. Did you forget to put the groceries away?" Jess questioned.

"What?"

"Oh my God, Adam, you didn't put the groceries away! Are you kidding me? I sent you a text saying to make sure to put away the groceries. You never check your phone." Jess insisted.

She was right. I didn't have time to check my phone because any chance I had for a moment of silence I filled with a new YouTube video or a podcast.

I looked over at the groceries to see the latest reminder of my costly failure looking right at me. *How didn't I notice those in between meetings? I mean, there were like ten bags on the counter, and I just walked by them? Maybe they're still good? Maybe it's not too late?*

"That was a huge order. We spent a ton of money on that! It's going to be ruined." I could hear the dread in Jess's voice.

"Maybe it's still good?" I said as I felt the tension rising in my heart. When you have a background as a military officer, it's obvious to those around you that you've been entrusted with greater responsibilities than putting away groceries. This type of stuff always goes back to just not being present. I look like an idiot. Like I don't care. And I have no excuse because she knows if this were something pertaining to business or the Army, it would have been taken care of.

"They arrived at noon. It's five! They're totally destroyed. Come on, Adam!" Jess groaned. "You never listen to me. Everything is going to be ruined, and that's our money."

I paused, thinking of an excuse. "I didn't see them. I was upstairs and totally forgot. You send so many texts that it's impossible for me to keep up with them." I countered.

"Really, what are we going to do now? We don't have any food. What's Addy going to eat for dinner?"

As I began to open the grocery bags, Nittany (imagine a dog version of Pumbaa from *The Lion King*) came charging in, spearing his head into the bags to see what he could snatch for himself. "Nittany, back off!" I said. (I love my dogs, but this was not the time.)

Glancing back at my burnt-out, frustrated, at-wits-end wife, I muttered, "I don't know. Maybe we can get takeout?"

"With what money? We just used the rest of our money to buy those groceries, and you don't get paid until Friday."

"Let me just check the bags, okay?" I don't know what was worse: knowing that I messed this up or her disgust. I was going to lose it. I could feel the pressure building inside of me.

Opening each bag and removing the room-temperature-originally-refrigerated groceries, it was obvious there weren't any survivors. Bag after bag, the groceries were all soggy and warm. The perishables had perished, the frozen foods had thawed, and the milk was spoiled.

I didn't say anything. I just held it all in as my wife spoke in the background. My mind entered this tunnel-like experience. All outside sound was muffled, but the voice inside was magnified. The weapon was condemning me, reminding me of the flood I had caused two weeks ago. Images of soggy carpet and water dripping from the ceiling filled my mind. As my mind raced back through all my recent failures, I could hear Jess one last time before everything went "empty."

"Seriously, Adam. What are we going to do right now? That's Addy's food for daycare tomorrow."

Maybe I'm not the right guy for the job. Maybe I'm not cut out for this family life. I just keep letting her down. I'm always messing up. Maybe they'd be better off without me.

As I turned my back to Jess, I picked up the last bag of groceries, grabbing the final casualty. Even Addy's go-to case of yogurt, her favorite food, was spoiled.

In the background, I could hear each full bag of groceries being dumped into the garbage. Money was going right into the trash because I couldn't complete a simple task like putting the groceries away. Because I just couldn't figure out how to be present.

I JUST COULDN'T FIGURE OUT HOW TO BE PRESENT.

Without saying a word, it was like time froze. Nothing moved. The dogs stopped barking. Jess stopped talking. My mind entered a deep tunnel of disconnection.

I just said, "I'm sorry. I can't do anything right. I need to breathe," and I walked right out of the house with no plans of what to do next.

I needed to get out of that environment. For the first time, I truly was out of options. No words mattered at this point. I couldn't live with the man I was becoming. I was always letting the girls down. The pressure was destroying me from the inside out—that constant pressure to provide—while I was obviously making things worse. I was done.

I had reached my breaking point.

CHAPTER 4

WANDERING IN THE WILDERNESS

At that point in my life, everything was clearly a wreck. It didn't matter how hard I pushed. I was just wandering through life without a clue. Jess and I had some pretty intense conversations over those next few months after the flood. Everything was falling apart, and I didn't know how to fix it.

I couldn't afford to fail as a father and a husband, and I was tired of feeling like a Father's Day poser.

There was no way I was going to waste my life, but regardless of how I felt, I knew I needed to change. Something was wrong inside of my heart. I didn't like the man I was becoming. When I looked in the mirror, I couldn't even comprehend the person staring back at me. It was like my fire was fading, but I wasn't willing to quit. I was going to fight for my family.

I knew I had to talk to someone I could trust. Someone with wisdom who knew my situation. Someone I didn't have to wear a mask for. So

I called up my buddy David Farwell. David, a full-time minister for twenty years, was a man I knew would give me the full truth. He was already well aware of the challenges we were facing in our home, so when I called him, we jumped right into it. I shared with him how stressed I felt and how irritated I was with who I'd become. I told him I was going to lose everything if I didn't change, but that I didn't know what to change. Just a few minutes after laying all my problems out on the table, I leaned in with my head low and waited for his response.

"Adam, you are going through the wilderness." He smiled. "But your goal is not to escape. It's to remain. Every great leader has to go through the wilderness." David explained. "In fact, God loves taking us into the wilderness. It's where all His best work takes place, and I don't think He wants you to leave too soon."

I thought to myself, *I'm sorry. Isn't the wilderness a bad thing? Did I hear him right? Did he say God wants me to stay in the wilderness?* This was foreign to me. *I'm not supposed to find my way out? Why not? I'm not supposed to just fix everything and get back to building my business? My marriage is falling apart, and you're telling me to take my time?*

The wilderness sucks. If you've been there, you know what I mean. You feel lost, confused, and out of place. You know you are wandering (possibly in circles), and you have no idea how to stop. You can't get traction in anything that matters. You feel like you're waiting for the next step, but you don't know which one to take. Everything feels foggy, and there is no end in sight. And to make matters worse, your family's patience is probably wearing thin with your lack of results.

"Why would God want me to be in the wilderness?" I asked.

"Well, first of all, before I answer that, just know the wilderness is not a time to build. I wouldn't build anything new right now because it won't last. Okay? It's really important that you know that," David said, leaning into the webcam. "This is a time to listen. In fact, anytime I've been taken into the wilderness, I find there is something I'm supposed to remove—a thought, business, relationship, or even belief that I need to leave behind."

> THE WILDERNESS SUCKS. IF YOU'VE BEEN THERE, YOU KNOW WHAT I MEAN. YOU FEEL LOST, CONFUSED, AND OUT OF PLACE. YOU KNOW YOU ARE WANDERING (POSSIBLY IN CIRCLES), AND YOU HAVE NO IDEA HOW TO STOP.

David went on to explain that God uses the wilderness in ways that we might not be able to fully understand or appreciate. He talked to me about my symptom of anger and reminded me that we don't treat sickness for the symptoms but for the root cause.

He helped me realize that the wilderness is not a place of punishment; instead, it's a place of preparation. If you feel lost and confused, this is a great time to see the opportunity in the adversity. I remember reading in Matthew 4:1-11 that Jesus was led into the wilderness by the Spirit of God for forty days before the devil tried to deceive Him. That had always stuck with me, but one day I heard a new interpretation of this event that surprised me. I've heard this explained in two different ways. One was that the devil chose the weakest moment of Jesus's life to attack. The other was that Jesus was preparing for a time that would require His deepest dependence on and awareness of truth. He was preparing to be deceived. He was preparing for the battle. Considering that, if the wilderness is used to prepare us, is it possible that God uses the wilderness as a training ground so that we experience even greater victory in the battles of our own life?

As the conversation continued, David explained to me that the gift of the wilderness can be used to bring about three types of adjustments—what I now call course corrections—to prepare us for the next leg of our journey. In the world of aviation, you learn quickly that within each flight, there are hundreds of microadjustments needed to keep the aircraft on course. These microadjustments to the aircraft are the difference between arriving safely and never arriving at your destination. I like to think of what David shared with me as microadjustments that made the biggest difference. These were the course corrections in my own life that were critical to aligning it for the greater destiny of both my family and my purpose.

COURSE CORRECTIONS FROM THE WILDERNESS

REDUCE   **REFINE**   **RESET**

COURSE CORRECTION ONE—REDUCE YOUR LOADOUT

The first course correction hidden in the gift of the wilderness is to reduce your loadout. A loadout consists of your weapons, supply, ammunition, equipment, and various other elements that you bring on a mission. In this first course correction, any unused or unnecessary equipment or weight must be reduced or removed. It can't go with you. Think about it. If you are carrying around a two-hundred-pound pack with equipment that you might use in a few months, wandering through some forest, trying to find a way out, don't you think you would start leaving behind what you don't truly need?

When I went through the Army's survival school (which totally sucked—we called it the best training you never want to have again), before becoming a pilot, I learned all about the importance of staying light and conserving energy. They taught us to bring only what we need and limit any unnecessary movement in order to conserve calories. Even after implementing the newly learned skills and techniques, in less than four weeks, I lost twenty-one pounds.

And the further I go, the more evident the benefits of following those principles become. Success is not about addition but subtraction. The most successful people are professionals at staying light and disciplining themselves to stay focused on their target.

SUCCESS IS NOT ABOUT ADDITION BUT SUBTRACTION.

If you are trying to work in the wilderness, here's what worked for me: I stopped building and started to focus on getting light. I reduced my commitments to other organizations, closed down a business, and simplified my life in any way that I could. If you are going through the wilderness, this might be the perfect time for you also to reduce your load.

COURSE CORRECTION TWO—REFINE YOUR RHYTHMS

The second course correction hidden in the gift of the wilderness is to refine your rhythms. Remember: if the wilderness is a preparation ground, we probably aren't going to go back to the same lives we lived because a new challenge awaits. There is something greater that we, as high-performing leaders, are being trained for. New opportunities will manifest, and priorities will arise when you get out of the wilderness that you can prepare for today. Life will not and should not be the same. Your rhythms are going to change, and right now is the time to intentionally think about what they should look like.

Quick recommendation: if you recently stepped out of the service, you'll want to make this course correction fast. It's time to refine your rhythms. Things are not going to be the same, roles and responsibilities in your home are probably going to shift, and it's going to take time for everyone to adjust. If you are getting back into the workforce after a time away due to COVID-19 or a transition from one position to another, either way, it's probably time to refine your rhythms.

Imagine a blacksmith sharpening a knight's sword before he departs for a great battle. The same sword will be used by the knight, but it is being refined. The impurities and unwanted defects are being removed. The damage from previous battles is repaired, and the sword is strengthened. The process of refinement allows the sword to become more effective and reliable for when it will be needed in the future. The same goes for you and me.

What worked for me at the beginning of my career wasn't going to work at this stage of life. I wasn't going to be able to continue working late hours. Scheduling additional business meetings instead of going home was no longer an option. And focusing on personal *growth*—which is a noble and worthy goal—to the extent that I was no longer *present in the moment* had to stop.

Thinking back to survival school, the literal wilderness of that environment refined me in ways I could never imagine replicating, but to this day, I see their effects. I am stronger, sharper, more resilient, and tougher. I value every meal. The wilderness experience of survival school refined me in that I can endure pain, and I need less than I think in order to survive.

With this decade's changes, many high-impact men and women are experiencing the weight of the world because they never developed the rhythms necessary to endure. Others achieved them, only to have their cadence interrupted when the pandemic hit. Weapons of mass deception exploit irregular or disrupted rhythms of rest, recovery, work, and play for both individuals and families. Refining your rhythms keeps you on track.

COURSE CORRECTION THREE—RESET YOUR COURSE

Finally, once you've reduced your loadout and refined your rhythms, it's time to implement the last course correction: reset your course. Most high-performing leaders do this too quickly. They don't take time to reduce the weight and refine their rhythms. They are so focused on fixing things that they either jump right back on course or pick a new course to follow without ever looking at the root cause, which is probably why the same problems come back even stronger than before.

This is why it feels like life is a never-ending rollercoaster. We're always reacting to the next issue. It's because, like me, you aren't finding the root cause in order to eliminate it.

This is why, as a leadership trainer, I emphasize looking for the lessons before moving on to the next strategy.

We can't treat life like it has a big reset button for indiscriminate do-overs.

That's just not the case.

There really is something called the law of sowing and reaping. What we sow, we will reap. There are consequences to our actions. But we can learn from them and use them as fuel for our next launch.

Look for the lesson that can be learned from that moment of failure. Ask yourself, *What caused me to veer off course?* If you can't pinpoint what it was or when it started, ask someone who will tell you the truth or help you backtrack. Then, reset your course. Either choose a new one, or move back to the original course.

LESSONS FROM THE WILDERNESS

When I look back on my time in the wilderness, I am surprised to say that I am thankful for all that happened. But I'm even more thankful that I didn't rush it.

I learned valuable life-changing lessons that I've remembered over the course of months and years because I didn't try to escape the purpose of the wilderness. As I reduced commitments, removed distractions, and refined my rhythms, my eyes could clearly see the weapons being wielded often by my own ambitions.

I share this conversation with you because, in order to define the weapon, we need to describe the weapon. Visualize what you are trying to carry with you that you need to let go of. Is it past decisions, old titles, or unforgiveness? What is weighing you down? What's overwhelming you? Are you ready to let go? This is your chance.

As pilots, early on, we learn the lesson of energy and weight management. In summary, not everything should come with you to the next destination. More is not better. We need to plan for the mission, bring what we need, and leave the rest.

> IN ORDER TO MAXIMIZE FUEL, WE NEED TO MINIMIZE WEIGHT. IN ORDER TO TAKE MORE WITH US LATER, WE NEED TO STAY LIGHT TODAY.

In order to maximize fuel, we need to minimize weight. In order to take more with us later, we need to stay light today. Society has taught mission-minded leaders to max out, load up, and do more in order to become more. Flying taught me the opposite. Flying taught me to release—to discipline myself to stay light because you never know what the next mission requires. David's visualization of the purpose of the wilderness reminded me of this lesson, and at that moment, the weapons became clear. I didn't have language for what was happening, but I could feel there was an attack on my heart. Something was trying to destroy my peace, purpose, and power. Something wanted to destroy my destiny.

WHAT WE SUPPRESS . . . SPREADS

I've come to realize that one of the biggest reasons our homes are stressful is—most often—because of us. What we suppress in our hearts spreads into our homes. I know that might sound oversimplified, and it is by no means meant to be accusatory, but I live by a principle that builds on what I shared previously. *We can only give what we have.*

We reflect what we've received from others. As leaders, we are the influencers of our homes. And we are the ones who can inspire the greatest change. It begins with us.

If that is true, then the best way to help our home begins by healing our heart.

CHAPTER 5

THE WEAPON THAT WAGES WAR

In *Star Wars*, Jedi Master Qui-Gon Jinn instructed young Anakin Skywalker with the famous line, "Your focus determines your reality."[13] How true that is, right? The stories from my past reveal that my focus was creating a destructive reality. I might not have realized it then, but the weapons of mass deception that I discovered in the wilderness were rooted deeply in my heart, ravaging the depths of my relationships.

Some were weighing me down, causing me to feel like I was going to explode at any moment. Others were specifically designed to pull me away, cause me to withdraw, and disconnect to create a life and a home that I would never have wished for. A broken marriage, a trail of hurt relationships, deep depression, and often feelings of a meaningless existence were tied to these cleverly concealed weapons of mass deception.

---
13 George Lucas, *Star Wars: Episode 1—The Phantom Menace* (May 16, 1999; Los Angeles, CA: Lucas Film, Ltd.).

Kris Vallotton, the senior associate leader of Bethel Church in Redding, California, said the following: "The nature of deception is that you don't know you are deceived. . . . That is why it's called deception."[14] Deception is excruciatingly challenging to detect in oneself because the mere act of detecting a deception means you have to assume you are wrong. As mission-minded leaders, it isn't in our *modi operandi* (plural of *modus operandi*) to easily admit that we are wrong. We are so driven by the dream and our reasoning that we just keep pressing forward, powered by our rationalizations. Just ask your spouse and kids. Chances are, like me, you're stubborn as a mule and believe that you're usually right. Which is why you're doing whatever it is you're doing in the first place. If there were a better way, you would be doing that, right?

I BELIEVE THE ONLY WAY WE'RE REALLY GOING TO RECOVER FROM WEAPONS OF MASS DECEPTION IS BY ENCOURAGING THE UNFILTERED CANDOR OF THOSE CLOSEST TO US.

This is why I believe the only way we're really going to recover from these weapons is by encouraging the unfiltered candor of those closest to us. That means we need to ask others to help us see what we can't see. Just like Kris stated, the challenge is that we don't know we are being deceived. Have you ever had a friend who is dating someone who you just know is using them? That person brings out

---

14 Kris Vallotton, "The Nature of Deception" wall post, *Facebook*, 25 Feb. 2014, 8:46 pm, https://www.facebook.com/kvministries/posts/the-nature-of-deception-is-that-you-dont-know-you-are-deceived-if-you-know-you-a/10151982357878741/.

the worst in your friend? But your friend can't tell because they're so infatuated? Do you remember having that conversation where they just get pissed at you and share how happy they are, but you know the truth? They're not happy. They're in a trance, but they can't see it. So you have to wait until all hell breaks loose; then you can help them see the truth.

This is kind of like that. In phase 2, when I start to reveal to you some of these weapons, most of them will be wrapped in noble, self-sacrificing stories, but when we peel back the layers, I'm hoping you'll see the truth of how destructive they've been. Or you can wait until the destruction is so evident—so vicious—that it can no longer be ignored. Your choice. One hurts worse. One is harder to clean up too, and I can tell you now that nothing but the grace of God got me through.

One of the darkest moments in a leader's life—male or female—is when they realize they are hurting the same people they set out to protect. With the constant rise of depression, divorce, and suicide, we must acknowledge that the mental battle is possibly even more dangerous than physical weapons. For veterans and first responders, this might not just be the battle with post-traumatic stress (PTS) but also a battle to overcome an unmet desire or an insatiable need to have done all the things you didn't do.

WEAPONS OF MASS DECEPTION ARE THE SILENT KILLERS HIDDEN IN THE HEARTS OF MOST HIGH-PERFORMING LEADERS.

Weapons of mass deception are the silent killers hidden in the hearts of most high-performing leaders. You just can't see them coming until the casualties begin to pile up. In the words of Mark Ronson and Bruno Mars, "Don't believe me? Just watch."[15]

All enemy weapons have an intended target and an expectation of destruction. The weapon is simply the transportation method for the damage that an adversary wishes to inflict on an opponent. For example, someone could use a gun or a knife to take a life. Both have the ability to kill someone. One might have a higher probability of lethality, but both can yield the same result. One weapon is better for close combat; the other is better suited for distance. Considering that, let's talk about the deadliest weapons ever created: the weaponization of destructive thoughts or what we call weapons of mass deception. Weapons of war that are unseen but even more deadly. Think I'm exaggerating? Check out this alarming statistic.

According to the US Department of Defense, from the start of the Iraqi War, to include the Afghanistan War, in fourteen years, there were 6,858 American personnel killed in action (KIA).[16] In that same period of time, approximately 73,000 veterans completed suicide.[17] I mean, how do we even process those numbers? Seventy-three thousand fathers, mothers, husbands, wives, sons, and daughters were so overwhelmed with pressure, limited by labels, and tortured by destructive thoughts that they decided to take their lives and remove themselves from this world. This is ten times the number of people killed in combat by physical weapons! Weapons of mass deception—caused by trauma, guilt, shame, addiction, mental illness, and the

---

15 Mark Ronson and Bruno Mars, vocalists, "Uptown Funk," by Mark Ronson, Bruno Mars, Jeff Bhasker, and Philip Lawrence, released January 13, 2015, track 4 on *Uptown Special*, RCA Records.
16 Casualty Report—Nov 28—*U.S. Department of Defense*, https://www.defense.gov/casualty.pdf.
17 Ron Self, "How to End Veteran Suicide," Filmed 11 Nov. 2016 at San Quentin State Prison, TED video, 12:27, *YouTube*, https://www.youtube.com/watch?v=IfG7WV-bN6Y.

list continues—were so powerful that people decided they could no longer live.

Can you see the dangers of the unseen attack?

The weapons of war are not just mobilized on the battlefield but in the mind and the heart.

If the enemy of a nation wants to destroy that nation's citizens, all the enemy needs to do is study the best way to deceive their opponent's people. Once they've done that, they influence their opponent's people to create contradicting values and beliefs that oppose their government's priorities.

Deception is often simply the long game to lead you into a world of destruction.

Millions of high-impact mission-minded men and women have lost their alignment to their true identity and purpose in pursuit of a deception.

Deception delays destiny.

Deception deters purpose.

Deception dissuades peace.

Deception destroys power.

And by their unique design, weapons of mass deception spread ruin into every stratum of life.

DEFINING THE WEAPON

The military has an entire publication dedicated to the use of deception. It's practically an instruction manual for fighting the enemy by misleading them.

The process is called military deception (MILDEC), and it's defined in Joint Publication 3-13.4. Military deception, and I've added emphasis to pertinent words, is defined as "actions executed to deliberately *mislead* adversary military, paramilitary, or violent extremist organization decision-makers, thereby causing the adversary to take specific *actions* (or *inactions*) that will contribute to the accomplishment of the friendly mission."[18]

That's interesting: "actions or inactions that will contribute to the accomplishment of the friendly mission." That means, according to the US Department of Defense (DOD), deception isn't just about causing someone to act but can also result in causing someone to delay acting.

Now, let's look at the definitions of the word deception from *Merriam-Webster*:

1) the act of causing someone to accept as true or valid what is false or invalid: the act of deceiving
2) the fact or condition of being deceived[19]

Bringing all this together, here's our working definition of deception: Deception is any act of hidden malicious intent that exploits another person's insecurities or motives in order to deter, delay, or dissuade them.

Now, let's take it up a level with our final working definition of what classifies something as a weapon of mass deception: A *weapon of mass deception* is any act of hidden malicious intent that exploits another person's insecurities or motives in order to *deter, delay, dissuade*, or *destroy* a multitude of people.

› **Deter**—discourage (someone) from doing something by instilling doubt or fear of the consequences
› **Delay**—make (someone or something) late or slow

---

18 "Military Deception," *Joint Publication 3-13.4*, 26 Jan. 2012, https://jfsc.ndu.edu/portals/72/documents/jc2ios/additional_reading/1c3-jp_3-13-4_mildec.pdf.
19 "Deception Definition & Meaning," *Merriam-Webster*, Merriam-Webster, https://www.merriam-webster.com/dictionary/deception.

> **Dissuade**—persuade (someone) not to take a particular course of action
> **Destroy**—put an end to the existence of (something) by damaging or attacking it

EFFECTS OF THE WEAPON

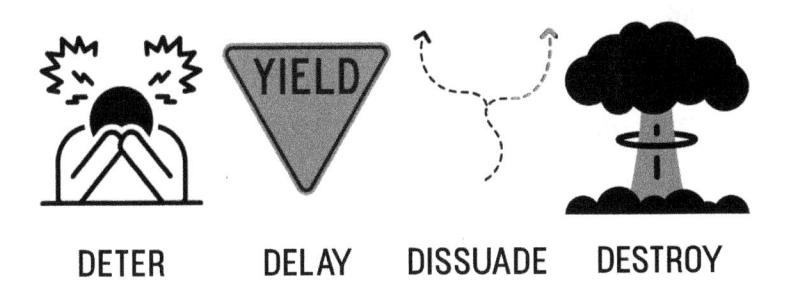

DETER   DELAY   DISSUADE   DESTROY

Weapons of mass deception are focused on delivering one hit that causes massive waves of damage—just like in the garden with Adam and Eve when one deception, believed to be truth, caused the death of us all through an act of independence that allowed sin to enter the world. If mankind had never agreed with the deception, how long would we have lived? What was God's original intent for humankind?

The weapons play on our motives and disordered desires to allure us to get what we want in the short term only to eventually destroy everything we love in the long term. These deceptions have been armed and mobilized against us to inflict mass destruction.

They will bring on more destruction than you would have ever imagined. Secondary and tertiary damage compound over time. When these weapons are mobilized against you, they will leave casualties on the battlefield of family, wounds in the hearts of your children, and loss in the lives of those who are connected to you. The scary thing is that you most likely can't see them.

HIGH-PERFORMING MISSION-MINDED MEN AND WOMEN ARE NOT THE ONLY TARGETS FOR WEAPONS OF MASS DECEPTION. THEY ARE THE ENTRY POINT FROM WHICH THE WEAPONS SPREAD. LEADERS HAVE INFLUENCE. IF YOU WANT TO TAKE OUT A KINGDOM, JUST DECEIVE THE KING OR QUEEN.

Weapons of mass deception are cleverly hidden behind a wall of mixed motives. Your chance of properly detecting them is slim. That's why you have this book. The weapons have been carefully concealed in your ambitions and strategically crafted to exploit your vulnerabilities.

If you can remember one thing from this first section, please remember this: High-performing mission-minded men and women are not the only targets for the weapon. They are the entry point from which the weapons spread outward. Leaders have influence. If you want to take out a kingdom, just deceive the king or queen.

The people will follow their leader.

If you capture the heart of the king or queen, you'll capture the heart of their people.

CHAPTER 6

THE HEART, THE HOME, AND THE HEADQUARTERS

Most people assume when a veteran or first responder is feeling the pain of a weapon of mass deception, it must have been caused by trauma. In my conversations with others, they immediately mention, "I can't imagine the trauma you all experienced from what you saw overseas." It's always said with great compassion but also faulty understanding. This leads me to my first point.

Trauma is only one of the four primary origins of this weapon. Hundreds of military men and women haven't experienced what most consider trauma—for example, seeing the death of a fellow soldier, surviving a suicide bombing, constantly receiving fire from enemy forces, and living on the edge. The people I've met didn't have those qualifiers to justify a reason why they were feeling the effects of destruction from the weapons of mass deception that we will discuss in the next phase.

I met women who were truck drivers in noncombat zones, men who were never deployed, men and women who didn't even feel worthy of calling themselves veterans because they were only in the Guard (that's me, by the way) conducting missions in the United States, women who wore a high rank but didn't see the significance of their jobs, and men who thought the military would have trained them for every future challenge in life, but without the uniform, they felt powerless.

Remember our working definition. A weapon of mass deception is any act of hidden malicious intent that exploits another person's insecurities or motives in order to *deter, delay, dissuade,* or *destroy* a multitude of people.

When we take time to see the consequences of a weapon of mass deception, it becomes clear that trauma is not the only cause.

THE ORIGINS OF THE WEAPONS

I trust that after reading this, you'll understand how susceptible high-achieving leaders and their families are to exploitation by a weapon of mass deception. You might even be surprised to discover that you have been affected by one of these weapons once you hear about where they originate. Here are four origins that I've discovered as the primary causes of a weapon of mass deception: transition, training, trauma, and timing.

> THE PRIMARY CAUSES OF WEAPONS
> OF MASS DECEPTION ARE TRANSITION,
> TRAINING, TRAUMA, AND TIMING.

Visualize these origins as traits programmed into the DNA of what appears to be a harmless seed planted in your heart. Over time, it begins to grow into a toxic tree that touches every aspect of your life. (See diagram below.) While at first, it grows only under the surface, eventually, it matures into a fully grown weapon that suffocates and wreaks havoc on the lives of all the people you love most.

ORIGINS OF THE WEAPON

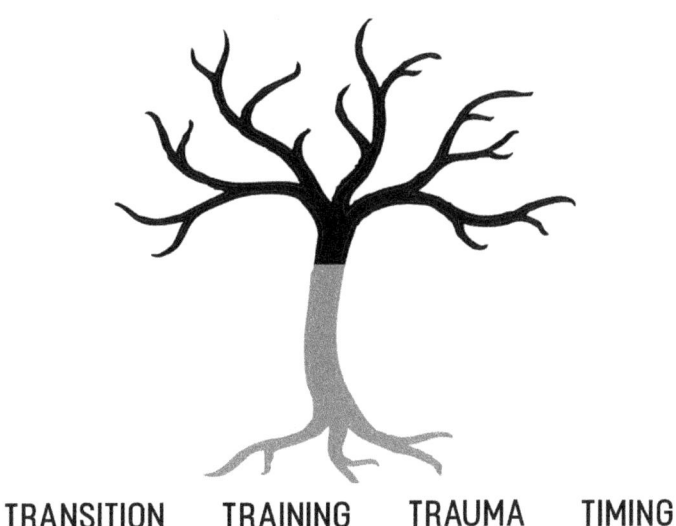

TRANSITION   TRAINING   TRAUMA   TIMING

Let's look deeper at each of the origins:

1) **Transition**—Job loss, moving, major illness, significant injuries, divorce, and death of a loved one are ranked as some of the most stressful life events. How many have you experienced in the past two years? There is something to be said about external stressors moving into our hearts. It doesn't take long for us to feel trapped in transition, to feel that we have no idea who we are now that

we've lost a title, position, or family member. I can't think of a more opportune moment for weapons of mass deception to start and spread than in the concealment of the changing of the times.

2) **Training**—People often miss this one, but I have come to realize this is truly the most dangerous origin of them all. In the military, I was trained to suppress my emotions because the mission required it. I'm not saying that's a bad thing. In fact, I think learning to shut down your emotions for a moment to accomplish a mission is critical. When younger children throw a tantrum in a public place or teens are hormonally emotional, a teacher's or parent's primary goal is usually to just "get through" the episode and move on. A child or teen may outwardly calm down, but there is no resolution. Even adults maintain control by ignoring or quashing their feelings for expediency's sake. The problem is that the soldier, child, teen, or adult misses the requirement to express what they were suppressing as they move further through the ranks, on to another task, or into another meeting. It's almost as if we are so used to running at 100 percent that we never allow ourselves to turn off and just be present with ourselves. And don't neglect the fact that we were trained by our families to operate a certain way as well.

3) **Trauma**—No doubt about it, trauma is a perfect opportunity for one of these weapons to appear. Based on podcast interviews with a former SWAT officer and an army master resiliency trainer, it's clear that many people experience trauma without ever realizing the damaging effects. One man explained to me that even just stepping out of the service, combined with moving to a new location and shutting down a company, can

equate to a traumatic experience for your brain. In fact, the National Center for Posttraumatic Stress Disorder (PTSD) reports that "about 12 million adults in the U.S. have PTSD during a given year."[20]

Trauma can be caused by many events, such as childhood experiences, abuse of religion, abandonment, neglect, change in caregivers, loss of a loved one, medical diagnoses, substance abuse, bullying, violence, or natural disasters. And what is traumatic for one person isn't necessarily traumatic for another.[21] So it's important we keep an open mind regarding moments in our lives that could have caused a traumatic experience where a weapon of mass deception was able to form.

4) **Timing**—Many people are overwhelmed by present and future time limitations. They simply feel they are running out of time. Often, I'll conduct leadership training for college athletes, and I'll ask the question, "Who here feels like you are behind in life?" The hands fly up every time, and every time, I'm speechless. Sophomores feel like they can't keep up with life when it's only begun. They feel they are behind and can't catch up. How is that possible? I wonder, Did you feel this way when you were supposed to focus mainly on school, family, friends, and sports? When does it end? When can we just breathe and enjoy life instead of beating ourselves up for what we haven't done yet? Forget mid-life crises; we're talking quarter-life here. If a weapon of mass deception can catch you at a time of life like this, you might never detect it.

---

20 "How Common Is PTSD in Adults? *Va.gov: Veterans Affairs*, 13 Sept. 2018, https://www.ptsd.va.gov/understand/common/common_adults.asp#:~:text=About%2012%20million%20adults%20in,100%20men%20(or%204%25).
21 Melissa Wither, PhD, "Not All Trauma Is the Same," *Psychology Today*, 8 Jan. 2021, https://www.psychologytoday.com/us/blog/modern-day-slavery/202101/not-all-trauma-is-the-same.

THE PATH OF THE WEAPON

Weapons of mass deception almost always spread into the depths of our relationships and environment following the same trajectory.

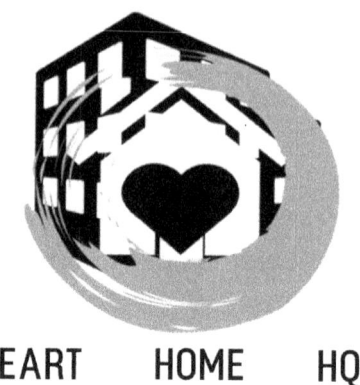

PATH OF THE WEAPON

HEART   HOME   HQ

We will discuss this in more detail during phase 3, but until then every weapon that I've personally detected seems to follow this path: it starts with the heart, then spreads into the home, and finally reaches the headquarters.

1) **The Heart**—What we suppress in our heart spreads into our homes. I thought if I just held everything inside that no one would notice, but that was the greatest deception of all. My suffering was not an isolated event. It was spreading. Jess could feel it, my work could feel it, and I'm sure my friends could feel it. My heart was hurting, but it wasn't until I saw the damage being done to those in my home that I was willing to change.

The origins that I described earlier allowed multiple weapons to form rapidly in my heart. I can't pinpoint what happened or when. I just remember looking in the mirror and practically hating the man staring back at me. Now, I get it. Basically, amid the newly detected COVID-19 virus that caused the world to lock down, leaving the army, shutting down a business, moving from Colorado to Pennsylvania, and starting a new career in a town where I didn't have any friends—all in the span of two months—I came under attack.

A weapon moved viciously through my heart and manifested in the way I lived. I had no idea that from within my heart, a foreign influence was beginning to spread through my words and actions into my home. My hardened heart no longer felt the compassion for and connection to the people in my life that I had always experienced before. It was as if my heart were overriding any sense of logic—until I saw the evidence: the dull, tired eyes of my wife staring back at me. She was experiencing an attack from the weapon as well. A weapon that was formed in my heart.

2) **The Home**—When we suppress what we are meant to release, it begins to suffocate our homes. That's what my wife was feeling. Weapons begin to do real damage when they reach this part of the path. Our atmosphere and surroundings respond to who we are. When we speak with a hardened heart or communicate indifference or apathy in our language, those in our homes begin to believe it. They feel the pressure that burdens us, and it starts to enter their hearts. If we are stressed, then everyone in our home begins to feel this stress. It's a vicious cycle that only intensifies with time.

That stress builds up, reinforces what started in the heart, and spreads into your close family and relationships. Not only that, but your family and friends begin to seem like they are losing energy and joy. You see it in their eyes, but you don't know what to do to stop it. In fact, you feel they are further stressing you out, and you just want to run away. This is exactly what the weapon wants you to think. Now that you've indefinitely suppressed your emotions, the weapon has spread to the home, and it's becoming firmly established in your environment.

3) **The Headquarters**—If we feel tension at home, we often bring that with us into the workplace. If we feel unappreciated at home—like we don't belong—we take that mindset with us to work, or we use work as a way to escape. Both are possible, and the weapon's devastation continues to spread but now from your home to follow you into your headquarters. The place that was an escape now seems pointless. The work you once loved, you have begun to despise because of what is growing inside of you. And if you slow down for a moment, you'll see the truly damaging effects of a weapon of mass deception. At this point, it has destroyed your sense of self, harmony with your family and friends, and the extension of your mission.

THAT'S THE DANGER OF A WEAPON OF MASS DECEPTION. IT FLOWS FROM YOUR HEART INTO YOUR HOME AND INTO EVERY OTHER AREA OF YOUR LIFE.

If you want to destroy the headquarters, start with the heart.
If you want to destroy the home, start with the heart.
That's the danger of a weapon of mass deception. It flows from your heart into your home and into every other area of your life.

If you feel stressed, your home feels stressful. If your home is stressful, your work feels stressful. What's the one thing they all have in common?

You.

If *you* want to change *your* life, start by changing *your* heart.

PHASE 1 SUMMARY

KEY TERMS

> **Weapon of Mass Deception**—any act of hidden malicious intent that exploits another person's insecurities or motives in order to deter, delay, dissuade, or destroy a multitude of people.
> **Continue Mission**—a common phrase in the military, also known as "Charlie Mike" in accordance with the phonetic alphabet. Continue Mission is the tagline of my organization Kingdom Operatives. It's also code to remind others to move forward despite the difficulties or achievements they've experienced because the mission matters. It's about resiliency and leadership coming together to press forward through adversity, no matter the difficulties, because we believe there is a bigger mission that requires our focus. We believe we have a purpose to our life, and we won't quit despite the challenges ahead.
> **High-Performing Leader**—the primary target of a weapon of mass deception because of his or her mission-focused mindset.
> **Blue Sky Leadership Strategy**—The Blue Sky Leadership Strategy (BSLS) is a leadership development method created by Adam Jones that combines a set of tactics, tools, and mindsets that have been used by high-performing organizations, military units, and executive teams around the world to create influential, effective, and resilient leaders by implementing three specializations:
> 1) Command Presence
> 2) Situational Awareness
> 3) Mission Readiness

- **Course Correction**—deliberate and necessary corrections to return to the greater mission for your life. There are often three course corrections taught in the wilderness:
    1) Reduce your loadout.
    2) Refine your rhythms.
    3) Reset your course.
- **Effects of the Weapon**
    1) Deter: Discourage from doing something by instilling doubt or fear of the consequences.
    2) Delay: Make late or slow.
    3) Dissuade: Persuade not to take a particular course of action.
    4) Destroy: Put an end to the existence of something by damaging or attacking it.
- **Origins of the Weapon**—the primary causes for a weapon of mass deception.
    1) Transition
    2) Training
    3) Trauma
    4) Timing
- **Path of the Weapon**—what we suppress in our heart spreads into our home and eventually reaches our headquarters.

KEY CONSIDERATIONS
- Ambition must be aligned to and provide availability for the accomplishment of our assignment.
- Extended service that abdicates our position of influence is selfish.
- Intentional conversations create transformational change.
- The wilderness is not a place of punishment but preparation.

> The heart, the home, and the headquarters are a representation of the progression of damage that comes from the effects of a weapon of mass deception when it follows the path of the weapon.

SUMMARY

We will not detect a weapon if we can't properly define the weapon. Language allows us to create a culture and train others based on what we have learned. If you feel you are maxed out, this book can guide you to find freedom. Most of the time, the pain we experience is due to ignorance of the root cause. This book will help address this directly. Additionally, we can only give what we have. If we have high levels of tension in our hearts, it will spread into our homes and eventually reach our headquarters. The weapon is weakened when it is defined.

PHASE 2
DETECT THE DECEPTION

"The war to end all wars is the battle for the human heart."
—Erwin McManus[22]

"Deceptive ideas play to disordered desires."
—John Mark Comer[23]

"The unexamined life is not worth living."
—Socrates

---

22 Erwin Raphael McManus, *Way Of The Warrior: An Ancient Path To Inner Peace* (Colorado Springs, CO: Waterbrook Press, 2021).
23 John Mark Comer, *Live No Lies: Recognize and Resist the Three Enemies That Sabotage Your Peace* (Colorado Springs, CO: WaterBrook Press, 2021).

PHASE 2 FRAMEWORK

Now, we are going to dive deeper and determine the exact weapon that has been hurting your heart, home, and headquarters. Once we do that, the hardest part is over. If I had to pick one section that would bring the majority of the answers you need to operate in the freedom you want, this would be it.

Knowing is half the battle. The strength of a weapon of mass deception is that it spreads with stealth. It doesn't want you to know it exists.

Here's how this section will progress. We'll start with a story to capture the essence of each weapon's effects. Then, we'll break that story down into some primary lessons. Lastly, we'll establish key indicators that we can use to detect current and future weapons for both ourselves and others.

Our only objective in phase 2 of Operation Restoration is to detect the deception. Nothing more.

At the end of this section, you'll complete a battle damage assessment (BDA) that will help you pinpoint the issues, so you can deploy a solution.

KNOWING THE TRUTH WILL SET YOU FREE.

This might sound easy, but success requires each of us to learn the lesson in the next chapter, so we don't waste our time.

Knowing the truth will set you free.

Let's begin.

CHAPTER 7

DRIFT HAPPENS

Who will you trust to call out the drift in your life?

"Sir, you're drifting left," my crew chief stated.

I didn't respond initially. It had been a long day and a long flight; my mind was maxed out. I was trying to hold a fifty-foot hover at 10:00 p.m. in strong winds after working a full day, and a medic was about to be lowered down a hoist. Not easy. Now, add the fact that we were surrounded by heavy vegetation (i.e. trees), and everyone on board, including the pilots, was wearing night vision goggles (NVGs) in order to conduct this mission. My vision was limited to what the goggles would show me. No peripheral vision is possible with NVGs, so it feels like you're constantly spinning your head around trying to see out of a tube. I was mentally exhausted, and trying to keep that aircraft perfectly in the same position was a struggle.

"Sir, you are *driiiiiiiiiifting* left," my crew chief stated once more.

Crap! I didn't respond fast enough.

"I know; hang on. I got it. These winds are beating me up. I'm trying to find a good reference point, but at this altitude, it's pretty tough...."

"Sir," my crew chief interrupted, "I don't care why you're drifting. Just fix it."

"Roger." I shifted my focus to realizing the importance of this training mission and that despite the challenges, I needed to find a way to lock in my hover.

"Holding position," I stated. This was the first step to correcting the drift—just acknowledging that I was drifting and stopping the drift. I didn't try to correct back into my original position; I just stopped the unintended movement.

"Alright, moving right," I stated my next intention. Now that the drift was stopped, I could correct back to my original position.

"Clear, right, I'll count you in, 5, 4, 3, 2, 1, hold hover."

"Holding. Sorry about that, man."

"It's all good, but let's take a second before we start the drop, and talk about it. I don't care why you're drifting. None of us do. We know the winds suck. We know this is a hard flight. But we've got to get it done and continue mission. Right?"

"Roger. You're totally right." I said.

"We're about to drop a medic from this aircraft. He needs you to lock it in. You don't need to explain why you're drifting, sir. You just need to fix it."

At this moment, I experienced a deep epiphany that I will never forget. It didn't matter what circumstances I was facing or how I wanted to hide the fact that I was drifting from the rest of the crew. They could clearly see my slight deviations in holding altitude and position. All that mattered was that I *was* drifting. He was calling it out, and it was my job to acknowledge it with zero emotion, shame, or guilt attached to that response.

Helicopter controls are extremely sensitive; the smallest movements make a huge difference. A hand movement of one inch in any direction changes everything. This is why we are taught to relax on the controls. We were constantly reminded early in flying to stop death-gripping the controls. Here's why: the tighter a pilot grips the controls the more unintended movement they create and the less smooth the flight will be. Want to know the greatest source of this? The tension in the pilot's body. In other words, if I get worked up, on edge, or nervous (which happens, by the way), and I allow it to transfer from my mind into my body, the aircraft is not going to operate the same way.

The best pilots I've ever had the honor to fly with were the most relaxed pilots. The way they spoke, the tone they used, everything was chill. They would lean back in their seat—instead of sitting upright—and carefully just make small adjustments. I remember one maintenance test pilot. During a flight, he said, "You're too tense, Captain. Just relax. Look at me. This is the pilot slouch. Lean back in your seat, and assume the pilot slouch."

So when someone calls out our drift (which happens practically every flight for the first few years), we are trained to respond with a calm and clear acknowledgment of that drift.

AS MISSION-MINDED LEADERS, WE NEED TO PUT THE EGO ASIDE, STOP TRYING TO LOOK PERFECT AND LIKE EVERYTHING IS GOOD, AND ACKNOWLEDGE THE FREAKING DRIFT. SERIOUSLY, ENOUGH IS ENOUGH.

That's it! We all drift. Drift happens. Drift is normal. But as mission-minded leaders, we need to put the ego aside, stop trying to look perfect and like everything is good, and acknowledge the FREAKING drift. Seriously, enough is enough.

Just acknowledge, first to yourself and then to someone else, that you are drifting. You can even say it that way. "Hey, I know I've been drifting lately." But you need to acknowledge that. This is what I had to do with my wife, but I couldn't acknowledge my drift *to her* until someone had the courage to call it out.

Here's how this normally goes:

1) Assuming you've created a relationship of trust and open communication with some people in your life, they might one day tell you that something is off. "You're drifting."

2) If you trust them and believe their intention is to help you, not hurt you, and the evidence is clear that something is off in your life, then you can say, "Thank you for telling me that. You're right."

3) Then you can dive deeper to see what is off, why it is off, and what you should do to fix it. Usually, if you are off, it's hurting other people, even if they haven't told you. So you'll want to tell them, "Hey, I know I've been off lately. I'm not sure what's going on, to be honest. I'm sure that's been hard for you. Thanks for sticking with me. I'm going to figure this out."

If you noticed in my example from the cockpit, I *didn't see* the deviation. I *didn't see* the drift.

One day, I met a great man who called out my drift. A man who changed my entire life with one statement. Over time, this man—Israel McGuicken—became one of the most influential leaders in my life and even my mentor. But it all started with him calling out my drift.

A drift that I couldn't see. I was tired, burnt out, mentally exhausted, and tunnel-visioned. *Sound familiar?*

Israel could read me like a book. After a few conversations, he said something I never expected. He said, "You're awesome man. The military made you so rigid and structured. Which can be good. But it can also create some damage. You're a good man, though, Adam. I can see that you are so afraid that you're going to get something wrong, and you want everything to be right, but I think you're carrying some real pain."

See, at this moment in my life, other than the building tension in my marriage and with my firstborn daughter, I hadn't even allowed myself to acknowledge a drift. I was too tunnel-visioned. I thought I was on track for success. I was following God's plan for my life, and I was helping many people in the process. I was speaking to audiences, coaching high-level leaders, and racking up interviews. When Israel called out my drift, I was shocked. I wondered, *What did I do wrong to show him that?* But then, quickly, I saw that he was leading with love. He truly cared about my health and could see a radical drift that I had no clue about. When he said it, I knew he was right. I couldn't see it, but I could feel it.

You know how, sometimes, someone calls out a problem that you don't even know you have, but when they say it, it resonates with your spirit? It's like your heart just recognizes the truth of the statement and realizes that it's accurate. Well, that's what happened at that moment. I'm not going to try to look tough for you right now. I'm going to be real like I promised.

Do you know what happened after that moment? I bawled. Streams of rushing tears and practically hysterical shaking started as he continued to speak about my drift. He didn't leave me there, though; he spoke into the truth of who I was—who I am. He shared with me the greatness that he saw inside of me and reminded me that I was a good man. I remember thinking, *A good man? Does he know how I acted during the flood? Does he know how much I feel like I'm going to explode each day? How can he say I'm a good man?*

But again, my heart said, *We need this. He is speaking truth.*

I had deep heart wounds from each of the weapons of mass deception. I had a heart that was hurting, but I didn't want to acknowledge it. The wounds were deeper than anything I could see on the surface. A deeper destruction that was so complex I couldn't process it myself.

This wound caused me to lash out at people I loved. To say things and do things that I wouldn't normally say or do. To live with annoyance and resentment toward complete strangers just because I didn't like something about them. To feel a pressure and weight that drove me to hustle and grind, despite everything going on around me. Just pulling me into a deeper state of depression and exhaustion.

My calendar was filled with business instead of family time. My words focused only on what I did and where I was going. My connection with God was only through the Bible. The joy, peace, and fun in my home were practically nonexistent, and, despite my mask of masculinity, Israel could see through it. Not only that, he had the courage to call it out. This man changed my life forever because he stopped me from crashing when I didn't even see it coming.

Because Israel called out my drift and helped me detect the weapons of mass deception in my life, I will never be the same.

I still can't believe it happened, but somehow, through principles and tactics that I'll share with you shortly, everything changed. My wife and I went from divided and irritated to united and on the same page. Our connection and intimacy are the best they've ever been. We understand each other, and we are all in for each other's cause and calling. She's become my favorite person in the world. There is no one I would rather be with.

BECAUSE ISRAEL CALLED OUT MY DRIFT AND HELPED ME DETECT THE WEAPONS OF MASS DECEPTION IN MY LIFE, I WILL NEVER BE THE SAME.

My connection with my daughters is priceless. Adalynne Grace brings me so much joy, and our snuggles at night make every day special. We read the same book every night. We sing together, pray together, and laugh together. I have never felt more love and compassion. I'm no longer a poser. And now, I use the story of my pain to help other fathers. There is a great quote from a pastor named Kim Clement that could not be more true: "Literally, your place of pain must become your place of reign."[24] That's exactly what's happened for me.

My newborn daughter, Aspen Faith, is receiving the best version of her father because he is healed. He detected the deceptions and dismantled them. He has been trained to catch his drift and has authorized others to call out his drift when they see it happening. I'm confident and intentional as a father because I have been freed.

Laughter and love fill our home. Business is thriving, and my fitness is back on track. We are always growing and on a journey, but I've never seen such a positive trajectory for my heart, my home, and my headquarters. And it all started with someone calling out my drift.

---

24 Kim Clement, "The Season of Multiplication," *Identity Network*, https://www.identitynetwork.net/Articles-and-Prophetic-Words?blogid=2093&view=post&articleid=24918&link=1&fldKeywords=&fldAuthor=&fldTopic=0.

Who will call out your drift? Who will you trust to track and watch your progress? My recommendation is that you find someone *now*. However, this is crucial: make sure they are vested in your transformation, and they will celebrate your success.

As we close this chapter, please find someone to call out your drift and even use the three course corrections we spoke about in phase 1. Deception is not always about getting you to do the wrong thing but, sometimes, good things in the wrong order. Your motives to serve and change the world are noble. I want you to succeed, but in order to do this in a way that is sustainable, you must first DETECT the deception.

DECEPTION IS NOT ALWAYS ABOUT GETTING YOU TO DO THE WRONG THING BUT, SOMETIMES, GOOD THINGS IN THE WRONG ORDER.

CHAPTER 8
WEIGHT OF THE WORLD

Surrounded by hundreds of soldiers, I had never felt so alone as I held my salute to honor the fallen soldier. I stood in shock. It just didn't make sense. It had only been a few months ago that I had seen him at my church, helping with the Father's Day cookout.

Standing at the front of the formation, my eyes scanned the faces of my soldiers, looking for a reaction. *How are they holding up?* Eyes of depression, confusion, and betrayal stared back at me. I could sense anger, despair, and detachment in the formation. Whose destiny was connected to this soldier's decision?

Specialist Williams had been one of my favorites. He was hard-working, joyful, and always seemed to find a way to take a mundane task and make it interesting. He attached excellence to everything that he put his heart into. So why this? It didn't make sense. This kid was one of the few soldiers that I would turn to if we needed to get the job done fast. I had no doubt he would fast-track his career and get promoted above his peers. I knew he would become a sergeant and a key leader in the battalion. He was a team player who dedicated himself to the service of others.

I remember, during one field training exercise, he had been tasked to teach a course on the basics of land navigation. Out of the nine stations and instructors we went through, his training was the best. As a company commander of fifty-four soldiers, I could see this soldier put his heart into his training course. He didn't look at this as a check-the-box type of training. He'd viewed it as an extension of who he was. He wasn't required to deliver anywhere near the level of training that he did, but he always operated way above expectations.

PERHAPS THE GREATEST QUALITY IN SOMEONE, IF LEFT UNCHECKED, CAN ALSO LEAD TO THEIR DESTRUCTION.

Perhaps the greatest quality in someone, if left unchecked, can also lead to their destruction.

I'm not able to ask Specialist Williams what caused him to take his life. From the outside looking in, he looked happy, excited, and hungry. Anyone can see the surface, but only God can see the heart. There are so many complexities to what leads someone down this path, and I never want to generalize or categorize someone's life and decisions. So, I will cautiously make this assessment. There is a very good chance that young man was attacked by the *Pressure of Performance.*

PRESSURE OF PERFORMANCE

I believe the life of Specialist Williams leads us to discover that pressure doesn't just produce diamonds; it can also sink ships. Pressure doesn't only bring out some people's best; it can bring out their worst. In our faith and in the church, we hear about how God uses pressure to build us. Yes, it might be true that He takes us through times of pressure to help us grow, but what about God placing the pressure to perform on us? I don't see that anywhere. I see that He calls us His child—His son or His daughter—and consistently reminds us that no matter what, He will never leave us.

In fact, for any of my fellow believers, I want to remind you that in the garden of Eden, we can see that humankind chose independence from God. Adam and Eve chose to leave God. God never chose to leave them. So what or who is placing pressure on us to perform in order to feel valuable? Religion, manipulative people, or many others—but not God.

Motives matter. Too much pressure on a home, and it collapses. Immense water pressure on a submarine hull will crush it. High blood pressure *in* a human can cause death. If we are motivated to perform for others and filled with a pressure not to let others down, it's going to crush us.

Stop for a moment, and consider the pressure you've been feeling. I'm not talking about the high-pressure situations around you but the build-up of unmanaged pressure within you. Have you felt that no matter what you do, it's never enough? That you're not good enough? That no matter how hard you work or how much success you have, it's never enough?

In the military, when we perform to a certain standard, we are accepted. When performance drops, if it drops long enough, we are removed. I fully agree with this practice for high-stakes teams in life-or-death situations, but if this policy translates into a personal belief system, it can be radically destructive.

I am writing about this because I lived it. The pressure of performance was killing me. I constantly felt stressed and tense. I believed that I was only as valuable as my latest measurement.

This is where the washing-machine flood that I spoke about in phase 1 came from. I wanted to perform for my wife and get everything right. Anything less than perfection was failure. The second something wasn't perfect, I felt it was pointless. Everyone drifts, but when you constantly makes excuses like I did, you can never just allow a situation to end with the event.

In order to feel valuable, I needed to hear from my clients how amazing my training was for them. And I didn't even realize that not everyone communicates with words of affirmation.

My worth was tied to my performance.

I didn't want to let anyone down.

I wanted to be accepted.

I was obsessed with receiving approval from other people.

I lived in my head. I operated in a constant state of intense pressure and anxiety that brought out my worst self at the most critical moments. I couldn't let anyone down, and I couldn't get anything wrong.

Until recently, I never knew why this was such a driving motivation, why it added this weight to my life. At first, this weapon of mass deception resulted in great achievement and awards. Pressure caused me to progress quickly through the ranks. I felt I was making God proud of me because I was always getting results, but inside, I felt like I was going to explode.

I craved approval from fellow leaders. Affirmations have always carried a lot of weight with me, and when someone, especially another respected leader, would tell me that I mattered and that they were proud of me, I would give anything and everything to hear it again. In my mind, it was never enough, but I thought if I built a big enough business or had a large enough impact, it eventually would be.

As mission-minded leaders who have dedicated our lives to the success of our organizations or the service of other people, our performance is constantly being measured. It's the nature of belonging to or striving to be part of high-performing organizations. The danger is that when we attach our sense of self-worth and value to our most recent scorecard, we will never connect to the place that holds our greatest power. Our presence.

How long do you think you can keep going on empty? How much further can you push in order to finally feel worthy of a reward?

For me, I was able to go back and speak to old clients and friends about their previous interactions with me. One friend, who recently interviewed me on his podcast, said, "Adam, something's changed. I have no idea what, but compared to the last time I saw you, you are not the same person at all. You have confidence, but it's real. What happened?"

That was the moment when I shared with them what I've told you today. I thought my value was determined by my performance, so I couldn't relax and be present. I just wanted to get it right. I didn't want to let anyone down. That belief had sucked me into the deep pit of depression, and I had no idea how to pull myself out.

WHAT I'M NOT SAYING

Let's be very clear about what I'm not saying when discussing the pressure of performance.

> I'm not saying that life is easy. In fact, I think it's actually very challenging. I think the complexities of parenthood, marriage, work, business, finance, and everything else only get more challenging. But challenges create champions.

> I'm not saying don't hustle or grind during different stages of your life. I think we should value hard work and dedication. I believe we should dedicate ourselves to causes worthy of our dedication.

> I'm not saying that your performance doesn't matter or that contributing to the team that you're on isn't important.

> I'm not saying to coast through life, allowing anything and everything to happen to you.

> I'm not saying to live in your comfort zone. In fact, I believe your comfort zone is your casket.

> I'm not saying to avoid situations that are challenging because you feel uncomfortable.

> I am not saying that organizations should lower their standards so that everyone feels like they belong. But before we measure someone's performance, I think that we, as high-performance leaders, must model the standard for other people to follow.

WHAT I AM SAYING

> I am saying that your performance should never dictate your value as a human being or your sense of belonging in life.

> I am saying that you don't need to live in a continual state of feeling like you aren't enough or that you have to prove your value to everyone in your life.

> I am saying that low performance in one area of your life that has caused you to become removed or disconnected from a community does not mean that you should carry that mentality into other places in your life. Just because you do not belong in a certain job does not mean you don't belong in life.
> I am saying that most of us have been trained by the world and by different high-performing organizations that our performance decides if we belong. It might be true for that organization, and maybe it should be true when it comes to working together on their team. Leaders have to protect the culture of an organization, so I get that. But if we aren't careful, we'll take that mindset and subconsciously authorize it to become a perceived reality in every area of our lives. (We'll talk about this in phase 3.)

EXTREME LEVELS OF PRESSURE CAN BE PARALYZING.

Extreme levels of pressure can be paralyzing.

In the military, we constantly enter situations where we must operate under heavy pressure. When an athlete steps out of their comfort zone and onto the field, they experience pressure to win the game and not let their team down. But to live in a consistent state of pressure on and off the field, during and after a mission, while you increase your core skills, grow your professional network, or advance your company is unnecessary. To believe that you are always behind and never enough is normally not in alignment with the plans that God has for your life. That is not how He designed you.

It's funny. I was consumed by the pressure of performance, yet I never detected it. Other people did, and they had the courage to tell me what they were seeing. I just thought most people didn't understand me. They didn't get my grind. They weren't on my level. But then, eventually, the right people pointed this out at the right time. I'm surprised they were able to even get my attention. I spoke with so much intensity (kind of still do—but it's a healthy level of intensity) and passion that I bet it was like trying to stop a runaway train that was close to running out of track.

Thank God they caught me in time.

KEY INDICATORS OF THE PRESSURE OF PERFORMANCE

Whenever I think about the pressure of performance, I imagine someone who is weighed down by the weight of the world, always thinking they need to go FASTER in order to be considered valuable by others. I've found that with all the weapons, there are key indicators that help us detect when we need to dismantle them. We know we are succumbing to the pressure of performance if we chronically feel any of the following:

> - Frustrated
> - Anxious
> - Stressed
> - Tense
> - Exhausted
> - Run-down

PRESSURE OF PERFORMANCE KEY INDICATORS

FRUSTRATED
ANXIOUS
STRESSED
TENSE
EXHAUSTED
RUN-DOWN

The pressure of performance can be detected by remembering the acronym FASTER. Simply put, if you are consistently feeling frustrated, anxious, stressed, tense, exhausted, and run-down, then there is no doubt in my mind that you are being targeted by the pressure of performance.

If you:
> Believe you need to go above and beyond what someone asks of you in order to impress and receive value from them.
> Worry that you are not good enough and feel like you are a fake.
> Feel the joy of an activity dissipate shortly after committing to it because you don't want to get it wrong.
> Live with an unending sense of pressure and tension causing you to act certain ways during stressful situations that you aren't proud of.

Then the pressure of performance knows you by name and is relentlessly compelling you to think the only way you will be valuable is if you keep going FASTER.

CHAPTER 9
YOU'RE LEAVING AGAIN?

Captain Brown was the go-to guy that everyone—everyone except three people—could count on. He gave his life to the mission and committed himself to a lifestyle of impact. His overachieving nature to direct and coordinate activities within the police department in service to the citizens of his city was seen by most as a badge of honor.

His unwavering willingness to volunteer for any mission brought him to the rank he holds today. For him, it was never about the rank anyway, but impact. He knew he was destined to make the world a better place, and he pledged himself to impact people he would never meet. He gave everything he had to make his life matter. Eventually, this go-getter attitude at work resulted in missed vacations, late and skipped dinners, long nights with no communication, and half-assed anniversary celebrations.

As he leaned forward in his chair, sweat dripping down his brow, he began to sign the final document. At his rank and level of influence, his signature had been required on thousands of forms and approvals.

Most of the time, he signed documents he would never remember. This one was different. Today's document he would never forget.

As his hand slowly dragged the pen across the page, he realized that he was responsible for this moment. He gave everyone at work his best but gave his family his leftovers. Oftentimes, this was shown through a disengaged blank stare while his children explained how school went. Or through his lifeless engagement when his wife would tell him what their plans were for the weekend. He was always zoning out and consumed by work.

Ever since he was a young boy, all he wanted to do was serve. He grew up watching movies like *Lethal Weapon* and television series like *Band of Brothers* and *Miami Vice*. This world of adventure, adrenaline, and achievement was everything he dreamed of.

Early in his career, after graduating from the police academy, he met his wife, Sarah. He met Sarah on the job. Within days of meeting, they went on their first date, and the connection was immediate. It didn't take long for him to know she was "the one," so he popped the question and asked her to marry him. She loved this heroic and selfless man who would give the shirt off his back if someone asked for it. His focus on impacting and serving others attracted Sarah. She loved and was honored to marry such a sacrificing and kind man.

Once Captain Brown made it to the big leagues, his career was fast-tracked. His drive and willingness to serve anyone, anytime, anywhere became his signature brand. Even during off hours, he was called upon to provide advice, and he never missed a phone call. He never set up the boundaries needed to protect his time with his family, and unknowingly his *yes* to another job was equally a *no* to time with his family.

As the pen completed his signature, his divorce was finalized. Something he never wanted became the future he created. He gave everything to everyone—but her. He looked up at Sarah's face only to find nothing. No emotion. She was over it. After twenty years of marriage, he was no longer the man she once knew. He had drifted away from her day by day and neither recognized it nor did anything to change it.

Her face looked tired from the years of hard nights alone with the kids. Her mouth was tightly shut, and her eyes couldn't even look at him. She was free from any more letdowns and unmet expectations. This wasn't what she wanted; she wanted the young man who had focused on the mission but also focused on the moments.

If only the man she married had seen the woman who needed him most.

Years later, Captain Brown is now Chief Brown. He has continued to level up and expand his ability to make an impact, but his kids barely know him. Even after the divorce, he didn't find the time to slow down. Despite his rank and achievements, he feels utterly empty. The life he wanted, he created, and he doesn't want it anymore. The impact he wanted to make has been fleeting. Those who know him best like him least. He's failed in the areas that matter most.

Brown was targeted by one of the deadliest and most common weapons of mass deception. He ascribed to the belief that the most selfless thing he could do was sacrifice what he loved most—his family—in order to impact the most people. By doing so, he armed the weapon that brought destruction to his marriage and relationship with his kids.

He sacrificed his family on the *Altar of Impact*.

ALTAR OF IMPACT

Have you found yourself on a path similar to Chief Brown's? It's not too late to detect the deception.

You might even think for a moment, *Adam—deception? What's wrong with wanting to make an impact?* Nothing. As long as you understand the difference between ambition and assignment and prioritize them accordingly. This was a lesson I had to learn the hard way since this weapon has proved to be the greatest weapon of mass deception for me to disarm. I'll talk about this in-depth during phase 3, but for now, let's peel back some layers to see what is so destructive about it.

We can sacrifice much on the altar of impact: friends, careers, joy, vacations, relationships, and the list goes on. For *Weapons of Mass Deception*, though, I want to focus on one of the most precious—yet common—treasures that is sacrificed: our families.

For some reason, we have been taught to believe that it is selfless to sacrifice the time and attention we naturally want to focus on our families. In other words, we think our greatest act of service is to those we have never met—when I believe God has assigned our family as our greatest purpose. Family relationships are those that we have the ability to shape, mentor, and transform in ways that aren't possible with a client or your team. Therefore, the altar of impact's influence can be detected by a growing distance in family relationships based on the drift that the weapon causes as we continually focus on everyone outside of our home instead of those most precious to us. Unfortunately, the story of Chief Brown mirrors the lives of a lot of mission-minded leaders.

I met great leaders in the military who lost their families because of their obsession and addiction to impact. Volunteering for every mission, deployment, and "extra credit" moment. I'm not trying to make light of this. Thank God for those who volunteer. In fact, let's acknowledge how amazing it is to live in a country where men and women choose to serve the citizens of our country—whether it's through emergency services, the military, or law enforcement. A volunteer army.

I'm thankful for all those who raise their hands to serve, and I see it as part of my responsibility to serve them now. The best way I can do that is by serving their families and bringing awareness to the presence of this often undetected weapon.

The altar of impact was tearing me apart. So if you are in that bucket as well, know you are not alone. I remember one day, my wife said, "Adam, you don't see me. You're not here. I don't know where you are, but you are not here."

At first, I didn't acknowledge the drift. I said, "What are you talking about? I'm right here. I'm sitting with you right now. Why do you always feel it's not enough? I don't know what else to do, Jess."

But over time, I realized something. She was right. I was drifting. I wasn't present. I was constantly disconnected from what was going on around me because I kept thinking of how much time I was wasting by staying home.

About two years later, after a lot of slow but steady progress in my marriage, my wife and I were having our date day, and it all clicked. I remember as we sat back and drank some wine, she said how proud she was of me. She said she couldn't believe the man I had become, and honestly, that blew my mind.

A tear rolled down my cheek as I said, "I can't tell you how good it feels to hear you say that. I'm sorry, Babe. I didn't realize it then, but even though you were right in front of me, for someone reason, it was like I would see through you."

Jess stopped, put her glass down, and said, "That's it. That's exactly how it felt. It felt like you were seeing through me."

Is it possible that you have sacrificed your family on the altar of impacting other people? Might you be looking *through* your spouse? Is it possible that this weapon has caused you to believe that your greatest place of impact is outside of your home?

For me, there was no deadlier and more destructive weapon that caused me to drift from not only my marriage but my role as a father and friend. I am here to tell you that if my drift could be corrected, it's just as possible for you. But will you acknowledge the drift?

WHAT I'M NOT SAYING

> - I'm not saying to stay on the couch all day and eat Cheetos and watch reruns with your family.
> - I'm not saying that your ONLY place for impact is at home as a parent or spouse.
> - I'm not saying this weapon is only focused on causing us to ignore our families. We also ignore our friends, neighbors, and even team members.
> - I'm not saying that you shouldn't set aside time to be away from your family to go help others.
> - I'm not saying that your voice into other people's lives doesn't matter or that it's not significant.
> - I'm not saying we shouldn't be looking for ways to bring transformation to and impact the world.
> - I'm not saying that you shouldn't volunteer or serve other people because you're only thinking of your own family. In my opinion, that's selfish. Don't you agree?
> - I'm not saying that you are intentionally sacrificing your family on the altar of impact. Most of this happens in the subconscious mind, based on how we are programmed in our earlier development (read phase 3) and through the influence of different cultures and communities.

WHAT I AM SAYING

> I am saying that we shouldn't abdicate our responsibilities to the people we are leading in order to expand and lead others.
> I am saying don't neglect those who have already been given into your care. If we place more of our focus and willingness to grow on work—than on our families—we have an issue.
> I am saying don't miss the moments right in front of you. Appreciate what's now.
> I am saying to train yourself to be fully present. Be where your feet are.
> I am saying a smaller-sized group doesn't mean a smaller level of significance. In fact, I believe most special forces organizations are called "small teams." Interesting?
> I am saying that we must not miss our GREATEST opportunity to impact the people who are placed right in front of us because we're always searching for who's next.

KEY INDICATORS OF THE ALTAR OF IMPACT

Before you read over the key indicators for the altar of impact, remember that a weapon of mass deception might start with you, but it's always spreading through you.

This means it's not only about you. Look for these indicators in your relationships and marriage. You'll need to slow down to see them.

If I asked you, "How's your marriage going?" what would you say? You would probably say, "Not bad, pretty good."

But what if I asked your spouse? Would I hear, "He doesn't see me," "She isn't present," "My spouse doesn't really help out around the house"? Or maybe, "It's been a struggle ever since he got out of the military," "All she ever thinks about is the next big deal," "He's always preparing for his next meeting or speaking engagement"?

In your role as a high-performance leader, it is very possible that you don't feel appreciated by your spouse or kids. I get that, but we can't control how they feel or communicate. You can only change your attitude and actions. That's it. Focus on what you can control, and I bet shortly after, you'll see changes in them as well.

Therefore, the key indicators listed below are not only to assess how we are feeling but also how the people around us are acting. It's hard to read how someone else is feeling based on their nonverbals, but you can see how they are acting. If you notice their DRIFT, chances are you should pay close attention to this weapon.

> Disconnected
> Resentful
> Irritated
> Fed Up
> Tense

ALTAR OF IMPACT KEY INDICATORS

DISCONNECTED
RESENTFUL
IRRITATED
FED UP
TENSE

The altar of impact can be detected by remembering to call out the drift. For instance, you might notice your spouse seems disconnected from you. It's like you aren't on the same page. Maybe you can sense resentment, and your spouse is quickly irritated with scattered focus and high levels of tension. If you notice any of these situations, the odds are that, like me, you have been sacrificing your relationship on the altar of impact, and its effects have spread to your home.

Due to your relentless focus and drive, you might have categorized certain activities with your spouse and kids as distractions. I remember thinking: *Dishes are a distraction. Laundry is a waste of time. Grocery shopping is causing me to miss opportunities to run meetings.* I couldn't see that these small things added up. I remember moments when Jess would snap at me for messing something up because I was wearing headphones while trying to "help" her around the house as I listened to a podcast. I was consistently prioritizing impacting other people and increasing my personal growth over the greatest opportunity to impact the people who were right in front of me. I was always drifting off into my imagination, thinking of what was next instead of what's now. I didn't realize my availability did not equal my presence.

How about you?

How has the altar of impact been causing you or those you love most to DRIFT?

CHAPTER 10
"ONLY A TRUCK DRIVER"

In 2018, licensed clinical psychologist Dr. Sheryl Ziegler presented a TED Talk called "Why Moms are Miserable."[25] It was too good to ignore. In fact, I decided to pull segments of her talk into this chapter.

I'm assuming this book is being read by high-performing men and women, but I think we all need to grasp how this specific weapon is influencing the primary caregivers—spouses and parents—in our homes.

In fact, my wife has clearly detected this weapon multiple times this year. For that reason, I'm going to shift our focus to hearing from Dr. Ziegler. Now, if you are one of those people who are about to zone out, shame on you. Wake up. You can't lead people if they don't know you care about them. This is going to get you bonus points when you tell

---

[25] Sheryl Ziegler, PsyD, "Why Moms Are Miserable," Filmed 15 Dec. 2017 at Wilmington, TED video, 10:10, *YouTube*, https://www.youtube.com/watch?v=MwvctN3Uejg.

your spouse about what you learned and how you never realized the social pressure that is crowding their headspace. By the way, before we read the segment from her talk, you should see the comments posted below this video (I've added emphasis) that has over 1.1 million views.

"I'm married with 3 kids and I stay home with the kids. Despite having my husband's income which I'm grateful for, I feel like a single parent because of the weight of the isolation and repetitive days. I love my kids to no end but simultaneously, I've lost my identity completely." (This comment has 1.5K likes.)

"It's not motherhood that makes us miserable. It's the lack of support."

"Wish I had heard this 26 years ago. Motherhood is draining yet fulfilling. I felt guilty for not being 100% happy about staying home with kids. Started drinking and hiding my drinking."

The comments just keep coming, and they are pretty alarming.

Here's my question: where are the spouses of these people? How are we creating space for them to share what's going on in their hearts? How are we supporting our families? Are we only focusing on ourselves and our needs? Because if so, that might be why our spouses can't stand us lately. They're alone.

Where are the spouses who can jump in, grab some dishes, and fold some laundry? Oh—I know. They are drifting. Look, I'm not upset with you. I just want you to see that whether our spouses say it or not, they need our help. So, man (or woman) up. Get out there, and change another diaper! (Okay, rant over.)

Excerpt from: "Why Moms are Miserable" by Dr. Sheryl Ziegler. (Emphasis is indicated by non-italics. The link to the presentation in its entirety has been provided in the footnote on page 117.)

About a year ago, as I was finishing my research on motherhood, I came across The Feminine Mystique, *written by Betty Friedan in 1963.*

The title of the first chapter is "The Problem That Has No Name." As I read through the pages, I felt my heart bursting.

I thought to myself, Every mom needs to know what's in these pages. *It helps give meaning to where moms were back then and where we still are today.*

Betty Friedan was able to interview these mothers who shared with her that they felt unfulfilled, alone and ashamed to admit *that they felt lost in the midst of motherhood. She called this the problem that has no name.*

The spread into suburbia, with its green lawns and large corner lots, was isolating for moms. Their worries over smallpox and polio were replaced by depression and alcoholism. Drug remedies, such as mother's little helper, promised relief from boredom, unhappiness, and anxiety. Sure, we've come a long way since the 1950s. But the feeling of loneliness and lack of fulfillment *is still the same today.*

In my practice, as a child and family therapist, I have heard a familiar story over and over of mothers who feel exhausted, overwhelmed, and lonely. I knew that I could relate to feeling exhausted and overwhelmed, but I didn't think that loneliness applied to me, or did it?

I thought to myself, I'm still best friends with people from childhood. I have a loving and supportive husband. I volunteer in my kids' schools and in our community, and my calendar is booked with dinners and parties. So I thought I was doing okay. Until one day, something happened that changed all of that.

A few years ago, after being in excruciating pain for two days, I drove myself to the ER.

Once I was examined, I was immediately admitted into a private room where I turned the TV on and settled in for what I figured was going to be a long night, and despite the fact that I was in a lot of pain, I was actually quite content.

I was lying in one of those reclining hospital beds. I had nurses coming in and checking on me. I had a warm hospital blanket on, and I was watching Sunday night football.

I had no kids to put down, no dishes to unload, and no laundry to fold. It was just me alone in a room, and then I had a lightbulb moment. I thought, Oh, I've heard about this before. This is what people are talking about.

I was having a hospital fantasy, a real-life hospital fantasy. And it felt really good.

But after I found out that I was having a kidney stone attack, the novelty did wear off.

And I thought to myself, besides my family, who could I call?

Who could I call right now to simply say, I am in the hospital? I don't need anything from you. No meals, no driving kids around. I just thought that you would want to know.

And in that moment, I realized that I was just as disconnected from my community as the mothers I see in my practice.

I had gotten so busy doing what all of us do. I moved around raising kids and advancing my career.

I was living my life in 60-minute increments going from school to soccer, home, and back to work.

I was feeling lonely, and I didn't even know it. Fifty years later, the problem that has no name is still with us.

It shows itself differently, but it's still the same problem.

Today, we have the rabbit hole of social media that shows what all the other mommies are doing better than us.

If we are a working mom, we feel guilty.

And if we're a stay at home mom, we feel judged.

We second-guess and stress over all the parenting decisions that we make. And all too often, we feel like failures and frauds.

Somewhere in our frantic and over-scheduled lives, we might have a husband with all of his needs and demands as well. Most of us somehow manage to maintain a career.

Okay, it's Adam. I'm back. What do you think about that? Is there any chance your spouse feels the same way? You'd better believe it. Any chance your parents feel this way? Without a doubt. The weapon of mass deception that is targeting our homes, sometimes through the hearts of our spouses, is destroying their joy. Unfortunately, we don't slow down enough to understand what it's like to be them. Some people aren't good at having conversations about this type of thing. I wasn't either. I was consumed with my own struggles.

My wife has been overwhelmed by this weapon in the past, and it continues to show up every now and then. It's expanding in the world we live in, and it's a weapon that is only becoming more destructive. It causes kids to doubt themselves and parents to hold their heads low as they constantly feel behind in life. It's a weapon that attacks 24/7 and becomes seen as just a way of life. It's the third weapon of mass deception, and it's called the *Cycle of Comparison*.

It's why some people always feel behind, overwhelmed, and lonely. It's why others constantly take pictures and post them to social media, hoping that someone will comment or like their photo to make them feel appreciated. And it's why many—unable to be present in the moment—are constantly planning the next event or buying the newest thing for their kids.

The cycle of comparison is stealing the joy out of every moment.

> THE CYCLE OF COMPARISON IS STEALING THE JOY OUT OF EVERY MOMENT.

CYCLE OF COMPARISON

In 2011, Bronnie Ware published a book about her time as a palliative care nurse.[26] She documented the five biggest regrets people expressed on their death bed. The number one regret of those who were going to pass away was, "I wish I'd had the courage to live a life true to myself, not the life others expected of me."[27]

What do you think causes us to compare so critically?

Is it how we were trained to aim for perfection?

Is it that the world teaches us what to do, what to wear, and how to communicate based on social pressure and cultural norms?

What causes us to see in others, specifically what we don't see in ourselves?

Recently, I went to grab a snack with my wife in Pittsburgh, and as we walked into the store, the owner asked me if I was Army: my tattoo is a dead giveaway. I said, "Yep, and you?" I could tell he had some military background, so I knew what the answer was going to be.

He replied, "Yeah, man."

---

26 Bronnie Ware, *The Top Five Regrets of the Dying: A Life Transformed by the Dearly Departing* (Carlsbad, CA: Hay House Inc., 2011).
27 Bronnie Ware, *The Top Five Regrets of the Dying*, 37.

We chatted about how long he was in, what he did, and how he likes being a business owner. Then, all of a sudden, these words came out of his mouth: "I was only a truck driver." I couldn't believe it! I had heard that same sentiment from, easily, two hundred other veterans and military members I'd chatted with over the years: "I was only [fill in the blank]." In his case, it was, "I was only a truck driver," but what about you? What causes you to feel like you didn't do enough?

I think for veterans, first responders, and other public servants, what we've done is never enough because we are always seeing what we didn't do, or we're seeing what other people have done. We are stuck in a cycle of comparison. As we progress through the ranks or up the ladder, we just compare ourselves to where we could be or the next person, a higher rank, or a better leader. Instead of being challenged and inspired by them, we just shift into comparison mode.

THE CYCLE OF COMPARISON STEALS OUR JOY. IT REMOVES ANY CHANCE OF FEELING CONFIDENT AND GRATEFUL BECAUSE WE ONLY SEE WHAT WE DON'T HAVE.

The cycle of comparison steals our joy. It removes any chance of feeling confident and grateful because we only see what we don't have.

When that business owner said he was only a truck driver, I just encouraged him. He knew I was a former captain, which is probably why he said it. I didn't even say I was a pilot because that would have probably only added to any sense of shame or regret that he was harboring in his heart.

Another guy I met said he was shot at multiple times as a convoy driver in the Marines, but he didn't return fire. He beat himself up with the fact that even though he deployed—even though he was a jacked Marine—he'd never shot at an enemy. And he said this caused him to feel like he never "got in the fight."

How many people feel that they didn't do enough and can't appreciate the small steps in the story of their life?

When I got out of the military, I remember telling people I had never deployed. The second I'd say that my shoulders would slump, my voice would become monotone, and it was like all my other accomplishments didn't matter. Who cared if I was a Black Hawk helicopter pilot and company commander? That's not enough.

One day in prayer, I felt a moment of certainty and peace that impressed upon me a message that I'm going to say was from God because I've never been more sure of anything in my life. At that moment, I heard in the core of my spirit, *Adam, why do you think I needed you to deploy? I didn't need you to deploy.*

When I heard that, I immediately saw the bigger picture. I didn't need to deploy because it wasn't the plan for my life. Could I have forced my own plans? Of course. But it didn't need to happen for me to become the man I was created to be or to serve the people I was being prepared to serve. At that moment, the cycle of comparison was weakened in my life. We'll talk more about this later, but just know that you don't need to feel this way forever, and neither does your spouse.

WHAT I'M NOT SAYING

- I'm not saying don't compete or attempt to level up in life.
- I'm not saying don't be your best.
- I'm not saying to stay comfortable and hide in your comfort zone.

- I'm not saying that other people's achievements aren't notable and shouldn't be applauded. Recognizing them doesn't make your accomplishment any less monumental.
- I'm not saying that you should not be competitive, work to grow, and become a good example for other people to follow.
- I'm not saying that you shouldn't feel encouraged by other people's growth and challenged by their example.
- I'm not saying that it's all about you or trying to help you feel better while putting others down. We don't beat the cycle of comparison by comparing different categories in our life where we're the obvious "winner."

WHAT I AM SAYING

- I am saying that comparison is the thief of all joy.
- I am saying that comparing your worst to someone else's best is not a fair measurement. You would never tell someone else to look at life this way, so why would you?
- I am saying that you could lead an organization of ten people. Someone else could lead an organization of one hundred, and they're both equally significant. One might have a further reach, and that is awesome, but it doesn't mean one life is more significant than another.
- I am saying that we should see the strengths in others, and we should tell them what we see in them.
- I am saying that we should unapologetically be who we are. We should radiate with a contagious confidence that other people can feel and are attracted to because we know who we are, and we know what we bring to the table.

KEY INDICATORS OF THE CYCLE OF COMPARISON

Possibly the saddest thing about the cycle of comparison and its ability to deter, delay, and dissuade us from walking in our purpose and connecting to our core identity is that it causes us to feel that we need to apologize for who we are. It causes us to lose the opportunity to connect and collaborate with others because we are consumed with feelings of inadequacy, so we operate with a mentality of scarcity.

We know we are succumbing to the cycle of comparison if we feel JUDGED:
> Jealous
> Unfulfilled
> Depleted
> Greedy
> Exhausted
> Distant

CYCLE OF COMPARISON KEY INDICATORS

JEALOUS
UNFULFILLED
DEPLETED
GREEDY
EXHAUSTED
DISTANT

It's okay; you can admit it.

Sometimes, you see someone else's success, and it only pisses you off and makes you feel more behind. I get it; I was there too. I thought if someone my age or with my experience had the rank, title, stage, or success that I was working towards, then it either meant that I didn't have what it took or that they were getting in my way.

I would see another pilot who had the same experience execute maneuvers with such precision, and it caused me to miss out on the pleasure of the flight. As a business owner working in direct sales, I would see someone else's success and only feel jealous instead of proud of their results. The next time you judge or feel like you're being judged, remember that it's most likely the cycle of comparison trying to stop you from enjoying what is. It's trying to steal your attention and cause you to focus on the 10 percent that's missing from your life instead of the 90 percent that's right there in front of you.

I know the cycle of comparison was tearing me up inside because I just felt like, despite any achievement, it wasn't enough. I constantly saw someone else's success and was reminded of what I didn't have. Instead of celebrating their win, I would distance myself from them. I wanted to trade stories. Now, I know better, but back then, I couldn't see past the weapon.

How often has your joy been stolen because your default is to see the gap between your situation and someone else's success? How frequently do you feel judged because you've made choices that are true to your heart but seem countercultural? Break the cycle of comparison, live genuinely, and relish that 90 percent.

CHAPTER 11

WHO HAVE I BECOME?

P rivate Jennings was in her golden hour when she first met Sergeant Eversmith. The man was a fast-moving, high-performing athlete who now proudly wore the Army uniform. One encounter told you everything you needed to know. His eyes constantly scanned the surroundings, looking to see who needed help. Once they acquired a target, they locked on with full attentiveness. He wore his rank proudly and knew the responsibilities of serving as a noncommissioned officer. He was ready to serve and sacrifice at any cost.

The firing range was hot. Ammo was launched down range for over two hours when it happened. No one saw it coming.

"Cease fire, cease fire, cease fire!" the soldiers yelled to the noncommissioned officer in charge.

"Cease fire!" the sergeant commanded to the firing tower.

"Medic! We need a medic! Private Jennings was hit," The soldiers screamed in panic. Jennings was critically wounded during a live-fire training exercise that had gone wrong. Expected to live less than an hour, her blood continued to soak through the gravel on firing lane 11. Her fellow soldiers scrambled to provide immediate aid as they prepared for the arrival of the nearest medic.

When Sergeant Joshua Eversmith arrived on the scene with his medical equipment, his eyes locked onto the chaos. Determined not to lose Jennings, he sprinted from his truck to the location, but already it seemed too late. Jennings could barely speak. Her breaths became shallow. She motioned to him to open her shoulder pocket. Inside, Sergeant Eversmith found a picture of her family. She had a husband and a baby. He couldn't lose her. *They* couldn't lose her.

He decided failure wasn't an option. He had to find a way. After an hour that felt like days, he was able to stop the bleed and assist her with her breathing. He gave everything he had to keep her going until they could get her to the closest hospital. Once she was carried into the ER, all he could do was hope that what he had done was enough to give the doctors a fighting chance. Jennings's husband, Kent, was in the ER waiting room, praying, when he saw Sergeant Eversmith.

"Thank you, Sergeant. Because of you, she still has a chance," Kent said.

"I'm sorry for what happened to your wife, sir. She would want you to have this." Sergeant Eversmith reached in his pocket to give Kent the blood-spattered picture of their family. Worried that what he had done might not have been enough, he felt a deep pit in his stomach. The doctors told him to head home and to get some rest, but all he could think about was the nightmare from firing lane 11.

Early the next morning, a call came through. Sergeant Eversmith leaned over to grab his phone and heard a faint raspy voice on the other end, "Sergeant Eversmith, this is Private Jennings."

"Private Jennings! Oh, my God, it's so good to hear your voice! You never gave up on—"

Specialist Jennings interrupted, "No—you never gave up. The doctors said the chances of me surviving were practically nonexistent, but you kept me alive. No one knows how I'm still alive. You were my miracle. Thank you, Sergeant."

Several months later, Sergeant Eversmith had finished his time in the military. Fall had arrived, and it was time to get back into the swing of things. He knew it would take some time to adjust to the civilian world, so he tried to keep things simple for a while. Before leaving the service, he had signed up for a few military transition programs and trainings to help him translate his skills from army jargon into civilian speak.

Eventually, through a website specifically designed to funnel veterans into meaningful employment opportunities, he was hired by a small startup tech company in the foothills of Boulder, Colorado. The hiring manager loved his background as a medic and figured he would work well in the high-stress environment of a startup culture.

Hopeful for the possibilities, Josh started his job. He wasn't too sure how his medical experience qualified him to be a database manager, but that didn't matter. All that mattered was that he would be able to be home with his girls for holidays and weekends all year long. A nice stable job.

Now, only one question remained. *What do you wear to a tech startup?* Josh thought to himself as he looked through his closet. He didn't really have a diverse wardrobe. In the past, he had worn the same thing almost every day. His options were usually Army combat uniform, PT shorts and shirt, dress blues, or cargo jeans and a polo. Even then, he had been told what to wear. As he scanned his closet, his eyes were captured by his Army dress blues.

A few months later marked the first snowfall of the year. Josh began to wonder what had happened to his life. As he reached for his puffy coat and gloves, he thought of his move from Fort Worth, Texas, to Colorado. It had been a total culture shift, and now, it was snowing in the fall.

Josh had found confidence in his decision, remembering that he knew it was time to get out of the military. He was willing to give up the uniform, the mission, and the title, all in order to be a more present husband and father. He noticed that his two girls weren't getting any younger and felt the best path forward for his family was for his time in the service to come to an end. He didn't want to miss another family event. He didn't want to plan a vacation, only to find out he would have to cancel last minute due to changes in his training schedule. He wanted to support his wife with her career. He had loved serving, but it was time to move on.

Winter was rough. Josh found himself drifting in all ways: staying up late, drinking more, and working out less. He couldn't recognize it then, but apathy and depression were rising within him. He felt frustrated that his life used to have so much meaning; his title and rank had given him a sense of significance. Without it, he had no idea who he was anymore. He couldn't call himself a sergeant, and his job as a data analyst had nothing to do with his background as a medic, but at that point, there was nothing he could do about that.

Spring arrived, and he continued to drift. He felt his best days were behind him, and nothing could change that. He felt like his growth had peaked in the military, and now he was only going backward. The life he had once approached with excitement, he now faced with anxiety. Freedom felt like a prison. Everything was changing, even the way he introduced himself.

How was he supposed to answer the question, "What do you do?"

Should he pick an answer from the past? "Well, I used to be a soldier in the Army," or should he settle for his current life? "I'm a data manager who hates his life."

He was constantly on edge. Everything annoyed him. He'd wanted this life, but now that he had it, he just wanted to go back to the world he once knew—to feel accepted again and to belong. When Josh walked through his neighborhood, he couldn't help but feel like the outsider. In the middle of conversations with other families, he'd drift into thought: *No one gets me, and no one ever will. I wonder what they really think of me. God, I just want to go home and grab a drink.*

A month later, the drift continued. Life itself felt like a chore. He could barely get himself to go into the gym and pick up a weight. Everything seemed pointless. He looked in the mirror and just felt embarrassment. He was an Army has-been: out-of-shape, overweight, and unmotivated. As he stared in the mirror, his thoughts wandered, *Who are you, Josh? What happened to you, man?* Sure, as an Army medic, he'd saved a few lives, but now what? He wasn't on the battlefield anymore, so who was he now? The guilt of what he hadn't done while serving was eating him alive. And while his wife, Ashley, could see it, she didn't know how to help. She just knew he was home, and for that, she was grateful.

"Josh, can you watch the kids tonight after work? I have to run some errands," Ashley asked.

"Yeah, no problem, Ash. I got it," Josh said as he looked away from his phone to answer her.

"Okay, thanks, Babe. Remember to take the steak out of the freezer. My parents are coming over around five, and I'm going to try out a new meal that I might use in the kitchen next week. We have this hugely popular chef coming to town, and I want to impress her, but I need to practice. So just make sure to have that ready when I get home. Okay?"

"Okay," Josh glanced away from his phone again. He was always trying to get two things done at once.

After work, it was just Josh and his two girls. As he tried to clean up the house and remember to complete everything on his to-do list from Ash, he kept getting distracted. Eva, the older one, consistently got into trouble, and every time he got started on a new task, he was pulled away to save her from imminent death.

"Eva! Stop going up the stairs!" Josh yelled.

"I want Mommy!" Eva screamed.

Josh knew that he was the stand-in for the MVP. His wife was the one who kept everything together.

His youngest, Nora, was just learning to walk on her own. Josh only glanced away for a moment to grab the steak when everything fell apart.

As she was trying to walk, Nora pulled the hand towel that Josh had left under a pot of hot water, and it poured right onto her leg.

"Waah!" Nora screamed.

"Nora! Oh, my God. I'm so sorry. Let's get you under some cold water, baby girl."

As Nora wailed, Eva kept screaming for her mom. Josh felt his blood start to boil. He wanted to scream but held it in. Myriad thoughts flitted through his mind: *Work sucks. My life is a wreck. Eva is throwing a tantrum, and now, Ash is on her way home, and I'm going to have to tell her about this. What the—?*

Right at that moment, Ash walked in the door. Baby Nora was screaming and being treated for a burn. Eva was upstairs—by herself—running around. The steak was still in the freezer.

"Josh. Give me Nora right now," Ash demanded.

Josh felt like a failure. His anger continued to mount. He turned to the freezer to grab the steak and a bag of peas. Trying to make up for lost time, he rushed to gather some of the ingredients his wife would need to make dinner.

"Josh, what did you do while I was gone? I can't even trust you to—"

Josh smashed the peas on the counter. The bag broke open, and tiny frozen green spheres slid across the counter onto the hardwood floor.

"Josh, seriously. What is your problem?" Ash asked, "Where are you going? My parents are on their way!"

Josh stormed out the door and jumped into his car

"Ugh!" *I'm done.*

Josh stepped on the gas. Captivated by his car's speedometer—40, 50, 55, 65, 75, 85, 90—he couldn't seem to break away from his anger this time. He was driving recklessly, swerving down back roads. With no end in sight or plan to follow, his thoughts began to race. *I have no freaking idea what I'm supposed to do. God, if You're there, give me an answer because I've never felt so lost.*

Right then, a coyote walked across the road. He swerved to miss it. The back wheels of his Impreza slid off the road, and he slammed on the brakes, screeching to a halt. The car behind him just missed the coyote and came within inches of hitting Josh.

What am I doing?

He just sat there in silence as tears streamed down his face.

Who have I become?

TRAP OF TITLE

Can you see it?

At what point did you detect the weapon of mass deception unleashing a relentless attack on Josh Eversmith? From beginning to end, it didn't matter what he did; he was trapped—constantly feeling like he didn't belong, and he wasn't good enough. He limited his future experiences based on prior labels. He was targeted by our fourth and final weapon of mass deception: the *Trap of Title*.

Confined and restricted by what a title used to provide, most leaders lose their sense of identity and significance without the rank on their chest or title to their name. This is most likely obvious to you, but it never hurts to be reminded that you are much more than your title. Let's deepen this discussion for a moment.

IF WHAT WE DO BECOMES OUR ANSWER TO WHO WE ARE, WHAT HAPPENS WHEN WHAT WE DO IS NO LONGER WHO WE WANT TO BE?

Recently, I was brought in to speak about leadership to a university football team (Let's go Bearcats!), and we discussed the trap of title in even greater detail. I mentioned that there are a few core statements that go through our mind when we are influenced by the trap of title.

1) If I don't have the right title, I can't be seen as a leader.
2) Now that I have the title, I don't want to mess up or do anything to lose it. I'll play it safe and try to appease anyone who can take it from me.
3) Without my title, I don't know who I am.

If *what we do* becomes our answer to *who we are,* what happens when what we do is no longer who we want to be?

I had to wrestle with these statements and questions when I discovered I was trapped by my title. And I finally began to see how my family was affected by the loss of that title as well.

WHAT I'M NOT SAYING

> - I am not saying that titles don't matter.
> - I am not saying that there isn't value in assigning titles and labels based on levels of authority, responsibility, and influence. In fact, titles and labels allow us to know whom to talk to and what their specialties are. Without them, chaos would ensue.
> - I am not saying a title isn't important to a position. Just don't give more trust to your title than your presence.

WHAT I AM SAYING

> - I am saying that a title should be used as leverage, not a limit. We can leverage our title to help others reach the next level in their life.
> - I am saying that we should see people for more than their title or experience.
> - I am saying to leaders that if you have people on your team with certain skill sets, attributes, and passions, you should not limit them based on a prior label.
> - I am saying that many people believe their title defines what they are capable of.
> - I am saying that leaders have become too reliant on a title to build their influence.
> - I am saying that there are multiple titles that could be interwoven to show the bigger picture of who we are.

> I am saying that if you want to be seen as more than a veteran or an administrator or an executive, then you must first see yourself and show yourself as more. Maybe put away the combat boots, Jimmy Choos, or black stilettos and the grunt style T-shirt, three-piece suit, or power blazer, and just be your authentic self. Just saying. (And, Allison Shapira, in the Harvard Business Review, agrees with me.[28])

KEY INDICATORS OF THE TRAP OF TITLE

You know you are succumbing to the trap of title if you feel like DEATH:
> Depressed
> Empty
> Apathetic
> Trapped
> Hollow

TRAP OF TITLE KEY INDICATORS

DEPRESSED
EMPTY
APATHETIC
TRAPPED
HOLLOW

[28] Allison Shapira, "The New Rules of Work Clothing," *Harvard Business Review*, 7 Sept. 2022, https://hbr.org/2022/09/the-new-rules-of-work-clothes.

Let's be crystal clear about this. Titles matter, and they are helpful as long as they are viewed as a reference for responsibility and authority. They do not define who we are or what we are capable of. If I'm sick, who do I need to go see? A doctor, right?

Titles are destructive when they are viewed as a limit or label that defines who you are and what you are capable of. This is why we call this weapon the *trap* of title. If you remember that the trap of title brings the DEATH of your greater purpose, then you'll never forget that this weapon is looking for ways to cause you to feel depressed, empty, angry, trapped, and hollow.

CHAPTER 12

BATTLE DAMAGE ASSESSMENT

Undoubtedly, you've recognized the influence of one—if not all—of the weapons of mass deception in your life. You might even be feeling the effects of one or more at this moment. So, even though I want you to finish this book, I feel it's important that you identify—now—which ones are affecting you and to what degree. Therefore, to see how much they could be affecting you, I've created a short quiz for each one.

Once you've taken the quizzes and detected the deception, it's sometimes best just to sit with that awareness. Take some time to think about everything you've learned—not just about the weapons but about yourself. If you're a person of faith, pray, and sit in silence with God. We still have work to do, so make sure you've gotten everything you can from this section.

To determine the extent of the effects of each of the weapons of mass deception, answer the following questions regarding the PACT on a scale of 1 to 5, with one being NEVER and five being ALWAYS. If the question isn't a perfect match to your current situation, do the best you can to make it applicable to you.

At the end of the assessment, add up the numbers, and give yourself an overall score for each weapon. Whichever score is the highest is probably the weapon you should focus on dismantling first.

When all is said and done, these questions are not all-encompassing. Asking someone to help you see where you are drifting or honestly evaluating yourself will be your best way of detecting the weapons. The BDA is simply a tool to guide you in our next phase of Operation Restoration.

Pressure of Performance

1) At least twice a week, you feel like you are letting someone down or getting something wrong, either at home or work.

    1   2   3   4   5

2) You tend to overexplain, putting too much pressure on yourself to get everything right and suppressing a deeper frustration in your heart.

    1   2   3   4   5

3) You cram to get one more thing completed, or you are constantly multitasking in order to feel you get enough done.

    1   2   3   4   5

4) At least 60 percent of your motivation in life comes from wanting to prove others wrong or to prove to them that you are valuable. You are often in your head, wondering what someone thinks about you.

    1   2   3   4   5

5) At least once every other month, you feel like you are going to "lose it," and you live with a constant sense of pressure and tension, causing you to act in ways that you aren't proud of during stressful situations.

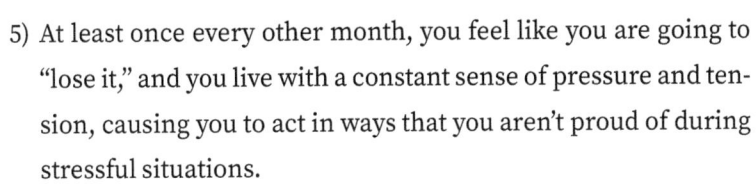

        1   2   3   4   5

TOTAL: _____

Altar of Impact

1) At least twice a week, you notice that you are staring at either your phone or computer or listening to client calls/growth-oriented audio after traditional work hours when you know you should be focused on your family.

        1   2   3   4   5

2) You find yourself saying things like "I have to go," or "They need me," as a reason to miss family events, and if you're honest with yourself, you feel that you are more appreciated at work or by your team.

        1   2   3   4   5

3) You feel a consistent struggle to connect to your spouse and pay attention to what they are sharing with you because it's challenging to be present. (If you aren't married, then choose someone close to you. This could be your parents, friends, coworkers, etc.)

        1   2   3   4   5

4) You know your employees, team members, or an equivalent are not getting the best version of you because most of your schedule and energy is dedicated to "new people." You feel the size of your following equates to the size of your influence.

        1   2   3   4   5

5) At least four times a month, your spouse or children complain that you have more time for others than them or that you aren't present.

        1   2   3   4   5

TOTAL: _____

Cycle of Comparison

1) Whenever you have a moment of success, you feel quickly deflated because you evaluate your progress and success based on other people's accomplishments.

        1   2   3   4   5

2) You talk down to yourself and seem to be your own worst critic.

        1   2   3   4   5

3) Most months, you find yourself saying, "I'm only a [fill in the blank]," or when talking about your past, "I was only a [fill in the blank]" or something equivalent.

        1   2   3   4   5

4) You feel guilt and shame regarding what you've done or haven't done in the past, and you try to justify your decisions to others.

        1   2   3   4   5

5) When you hear about someone else's success in a situation similar to yours, instead of getting motivated and inspired, you feel contempt or jealousy.

        1   2   3   4   5

TOTAL: _____

Trap of Title

1) You feel like you have lost yourself and your purpose without your title and position at work. (If you haven't experienced this loss yet, how do you think you would respond?)

    1   2   3   4   5

2) You normally refer to yourself by your occupation when it comes to meeting other people.

    1   2   3   4   5

3) You feel like, regardless of any accomplishments in your life, it's never enough and that you are only happy or excited for a few moments before the feeling fades away.

    1   2   3   4   5

4) You feel your position is constantly in jeopardy. You want to make bolder comments and more confident decisions, but you are afraid to muddy the waters.

    1   2   3   4   5

5) Your confidence ebbs and flows based on where you are. You are more confident at work or with your team than anywhere else.

    1   2   3   4   5

TOTAL: _____

PHASE 2 SUMMARY

KEY TERMS

> **Key Indicator**—an exhibited trend of feelings/behaviors that indicates the extent a weapon of mass deception is influencing us or those we love
> **Pressure of Performance**—The tendency to assign an overwhelming level of importance to proving one's inherent value or belonging based on their ability to produce. This weapon is best detected by noticing if someone consistently appears frustrated, anxious, stressed, tense, exhausted, or run-down. (FASTER)
> **Altar of Impact**—The place on which people sacrifice their current relationships for outward effect. This weapon is best detected by noticing if someone consistently appears disconnected, resentful, irritated, fed up, or tense. (DRIFT)
> **Cycle of Comparison**—The repetitive and continual examination of one person's weaknesses against another person's strengths. This weapon is best detected by noticing if someone consistently appears jealous, unfulfilled, depleted, greedy, exhausted, or distant. (JUDGED)
> **Trap of Title**—A thought process that inhibits someone's progression based on their dependence on a label. This weapon is best detected by noticing if someone consistently appears depressed, empty, angry, trapped, or hollow. (DEATH)
> **Battle Damage Assessment**—a tool to assess damage inflicted on a target.

KEY CONSIDERATIONS

> Deception is not always about getting a person to do the wrong thing. Sometimes they do the right thing in the wrong order. John Mark Comer explains how deceptive ideas lead to disordered desires in his book Live No Lies.29
> Steps to correct the Drift:
> 1) Call out the drift.
> 2) Acknowledge the drift.
> 3) Stop the drift.
> 4) Announce your intentions.
> 5) Move back to the intended course or location.
> 6) Hold your position.

SUMMARY

Anyone who is ambitious and mission-minded is susceptible to an attack from any of the four weapons of mass deception. The most critical step to destroying the influence of these weapons is to accurately detect them. This section provides the language needed to clearly connect the damage you've found to the weapon that has caused it. If it's been a challenge for you to talk about how you feel and what you are struggling with, consider showing a page or two to the people in your life who need to know. You can simply say, "Hey, I know we've been going through a lot lately. I'm reading this book that I think describes what I'm noticing and probably what you've noticed. Can you read this real quick? I think it's going to help us."

---

29 John Mark Comer, *Live No Lies: Recognize and Resist the Three Enemies That Sabotage Your Peace* (Grand Rapids, MI: Harper Christian Resources, 2022).

PHASE 3

DISMANTLE THE WEAPON

"You are not a victim. You can control your reactions. You do have a choice."
—Caroline Leaf, *Switch On Your Brain*[30]

---

30 Caroline Leaf, *Switch on Your Brain: The Key to Peak Happiness, Thinking, and Health* (Grand Rapids, MI: Baker Books, 2015).

PHASE 3 FRAMEWORK

Now that we have defined the weapon and detected the deception, it's time to dismantle the weapon and destroy its influence in your life. It will take some work, but as long as you have acknowledged the drift, you have everything you need to complete this process. It may seem like your world is falling apart, but you can do this. There is a bigger mission that requires your focus.

In this section, we will talk about a key practice that worked for me. I believe it will help you identify the patterns you fall into when the weapons are at work. Once you identify the patterns and dismantle the weapons, you can redesign new patterns. Over time, you might develop other ways to attack the influence of the weapons, but this will get you started.

Ready to roll? Then, as I mentioned in the Phase 1 Summary . . . Charlie Mike. Let's *Continue Mission*.

CHAPTER 13

TRUST YOUR INSTRUMENTS

To the east of the Rocky Mountains is an endless series of flat plains and highways connecting cities and towns such as Denver, Fort Collins, and Boulder throughout Colorado. The weather report stated low cloud ceiling, light turbulence, and low visibility. These were perfect conditions for training on our instrument flight procedures.

After about an hour of flying in the clouds, we encountered an issue.

"Captain Jones, our aircraft is descending at 500 feet per minute and banking left," said the pilot in command (PC).

"We are? I feel completely level right now, Chief." I said.

"Yeah, it doesn't matter how you feel, sir. Check your instruments."

"Woah! You're right," I said as I checked my first two instruments: the vertical speed indicator showing the descent and the attitude indicator showing the wings in a turn.

"Executing unusual attitude recovery," I announced to the crew, stating my intent and the procedure that we would follow to correct the issue.

Next, I glanced at the horizontal situation indicator, and it showed a deviation from the planned heading. *I'm off course. Gotta fix that, but one thing at a time.*

Once the aircraft was level, I felt terribly unbalanced. Humans maintain their spatial orientation based on what they see, hear, and feel on the ground. Remove the ground—like you do in an aircraft—and a person's normal senses easily become disoriented. An overwhelming sensation began to throw me back into my seat. It felt like I was going to fall out of the aircraft.

"I have the leans, Chief. But I'm okay to keep flying. Back me up on the controls," I said.

I was experiencing a vestibular illusion called the leans. It's another form of spatial disorientation that we trained for in the simulators, but this time it was real. Just seconds ago, I was descending and turning to the left, but everything in my body felt level. Now that the aircraft was actually level, I felt like I was descending and turning to the left. Every part of me didn't want to keep the aircraft level because it felt like I was going against reality. It didn't matter how I felt. I had to trust my instruments.

"Roger, with you on the controls," he stated.

"Roger."

I continued my scan to my fourth instrument, the torque gauge, and noticed that we had just about 15 percent more power left until we would hit an aircraft limitation.

The most important part of recovering from an unusual attitude is knowing which corrections to make first, so despite the rapid fall, I had to wait to check my airspeed before I would pull in any additional power.

"Airspeed is twenty knots over. Correcting airspeed." I was glad I waited because once I slowed down, the aircraft naturally started to fix the altitude during forward flight since the slower you go, the less power it takes, unless you are in a hover, but that's a story for another time.

"Decelerating airspeed," I said as I pulled back to decrease the airspeed, still feeling like I was going to fall out of the aircraft from the ongoing effects of the leans.

"Reducing power," I said a few seconds later, reducing the power to adjust for the slower airspeed and a rapid climb.

"Roger. Looking good," he said.

"Setting torque back to cruise setting," I said as we reached our desired altitude, and I adjusted the power once more.

"Aircraft in trim," and I pressed the pedal and adjusted the tail rotor.

"Fixing heading, turning back on course."

"Looks like we are back on track. Thanks for calling that out and backing me up," I acknowledged after the procedure was complete, and the aircraft was back on track. The effects of the leans were wearing off, and my body could finally recognize the truth of the aircraft's position. Only after leveling out the aircraft, correcting the airspeed, setting the power, and putting the aircraft back in trim—in that order—could I turn us back to our intended course.

"Nice job, sir. That was a good learning experience for you. Always trust your instruments."

UNDERSTANDING THE FOUR KEYS TO CORRECTION

The process of recovering from an unusual attitude and the leans can be overwhelming. Similar to detecting and disarming each of the weapons of mass deception, there are some core lessons we need to unpack. For the rest of this chapter, we're going to lay the foundation and put beliefs in place in order to disarm the unspoken, hidden agreements you've made with each weapon.

Many leaders fail to detect deception until it's almost too late. They're not aware of the indicators to watch for as we discussed previously. This example from the cockpit is meant to help you remember the four keys to detect and correct at the onset of deception. We call these the *Four Keys to Correction*.

FOUR KEYS TO CORRECTION

1. TRUST YOUR INSTRUMENTS
2. TRAINING IS CRITICAL AND ORDER MATTERS
3. EVERYTHING IS CONNECTED
4. EACH ACTION SHOULD BE SMOOTH, COORDINATED, AND DELIBERATE

Once you know what you're looking for, you can easily implement countermeasures.

1) **Trust**—Our feelings might be wrong. We must trust our instruments and the experience of the leaders around us. If I had continued to trust my feelings or the pilot in command hadn't called out the deviation, it would have been catastrophic. Sometimes,

as high-performance leaders, we put more confidence in how we feel than the evidence—the measurements of our instruments. Our ego and pride get in our way, blocking our ability to see the signs.

2) **Training**—Training is critical, and order matters. We must correct the issue in the right order. The only reason I knew the procedures to correct this issue was because we trained for them—not once, not twice, not just in flight school, but before every single flight. Procedure called for us to announce how we would recover from an unusual attitude and spatial disorientation. The reason we consistently rehearsed this procedure is not because it was common but because it was deadly. It's one of the most unforgiving situations a flight crew could face. Additionally, the order in which we execute each movement matters. I was descending; wouldn't it have made sense to pull power first? For an untrained pilot, that is exactly what would have happened, and it might have magnified the issue. Had I done so, I would have most likely hit a power limitation and created more problems for us to deal with.

3) **Connection**—Everything is connected. For every action, there is a reaction. The funny thing about flying a helicopter—even more than an airplane—is that the aircraft has some odd ways of responding to your actions. For instance, let's talk about pulling the aircraft up off the ground into a hover.

Imagine for a moment we are in the cockpit together. The rotor disc is at full operating speed and turning clockwise. As the blades cut through the air, I announce we are going to come up to a ten-foot hover. Slowly and deliberately, I pull power and lift the aircraft off the ground. Immediately, the nose of the aircraft begins to turn instead of pointing forward. Why? Because every action has a reaction. The rotor disc is turning clockwise, so when the wheels of the aircraft are lifted off the ground, the body of the aircraft begins to turn counterclockwise. Not only that, but the power applied causes the aircraft to drift backward because as I pulled power, the rotor disc tilted slightly back. Additionally, we are starting to roll slightly to the left. All of this needs to be corrected in order to just have the aircraft point forward and hover at your desired altitude. Sounds fun, right?

All we did was pull power to hover the aircraft, but because every action has a reaction, we were starting to spin left, tip backward, and roll left. In order to counter this, you need to do the following: push a little bit on the left pedal (to adjust the tail rotor and point the nose straight), then apply counter pressure with the right pedal (don't want to overcorrect), slightly push the nose down and to the right with the cyclic (pitch) to stop from drifting backward and rolling over, adjust your power slightly to hold your hover, and make all the necessary corrections again every time you touch the power while hovering the aircraft. All of that has to happen just to hover an aircraft. It's all connected.

4) **Intentionality**—Each corrective action should be smooth, coordinated, and deliberate. We must be intentional. Let's say that when the PC announced the issue, I would have just yanked the power, banked a turn in the opposite direction, slammed on the pedal to fix the trim, and tried to get back on course all at once. This might have looked cool in a movie, and there are moments when the mission might require that we fly like this, but in this situation, I would have been overcorrecting the aircraft. If I had done that, the pilot in command would have

most likely jumped on the controls and told me he was flying because I had just scared the living crap out of him. Additionally, the overcorrection could rapidly have led into rolling the aircraft and, most likely, a catastrophic crash. An unintended deviation would have progressed into an unrecoverable aircraft emergency.

APPLYING THE FOUR KEYS TO CORRECTION

Now, let's apply the Four Keys to Correction to your life.

To start, are you descending, climbing, drifting off course, or on track? Says who? Based on what? What does level flight for your life look like? Are you just going by how you feel? Are you listening to your ego? Who says you're on track?

Here are some ways to apply the Four Keys to Correction:

Trust Your Instruments

First, *your feelings might be wrong. We must trust our instruments and the experience of leaders around us.* You might think things are fine, but if you asked your spouse if you are on the right course, what drift would you discover? How about your son? Would he say Dad is his hero right now? Would your daughter say she feels loved by you? No condemnation, but sometimes we need to wake up and see the signs right in front of us. We need to trust our instruments.

And just a thought: your feelings might be wrong. This is an example of the power and destruction that can come from a weapon of mass deception that is undetected or ignored. These weapons are cleverly concealed, often hidden in people's motives while exploiting their noble intentions. Weapons of mass deception will lead you down a path that seems to be on target, but slowly, these weapons will begin to either *drag you down or draw you away* from what matters most. If we don't *trust our instruments* that provide us with clear evidence, then over time, it will, without a doubt, lead to destruction. Without an instrument panel, you can't identify reality.

Order Is As Critical As Training

Second, *training is critical, and order matters. We must correct the issues in the right order.* Deception isn't just about doing the wrong thing. Like I mentioned earlier, it's often doing the right thing in the wrong order. It's that simple. If weapons of mass deception can entice you just enough to get your priorities out of alignment, then they can guide you.

DECEPTION ISN'T JUST ABOUT DOING THE WRONG THING. IT'S OFTEN DOING THE RIGHT THING IN THE WRONG ORDER.

Think about it this way. Let's say you have been searching for motivation since leaving the military or your last position. You really feel like you are missing a sense of meaning and belonging in life. Eventually, you find a community that makes you feel alive. You give everything to that community. You show up early and stay late. You regain your motivation based on this activity and community. That's great! There was a moment when you felt like you didn't know who you were without the uniform or the title, but the search has ended. You're all better.

But here's the issue. Once again, you've found your identity and motivation in *what you do* instead of *who you are*. Initially, your motivation dropped because you didn't know who you were and what you brought to the table. Now, this radical lifestyle of fitness might be helping your body, but it's most likely only dealing with the symptom. A few years pass, and after a life-changing injury or setback, you can no longer train your body or wield your mind like you used to, and once again, the motivation is gone.

The weapon has pulled you from your destiny and pushed you into a deeper pit of depression because you didn't get the order right. Instead of starting by connecting to a mission and fighting to discover who you are, you only found motivation from a new activity. The order matters. I'm convinced that when you first find a compelling mission, you'll discover lasting motivation. You'll learn who you are and what you can offer because the mission will draw you in and reveal your core identity.

Everything is Connected

Third, *everything is connected. For every action, there is a reaction.* For all the prior first responders out there, when you were at an academy, you had to participate in mandatory physical training. It was scheduled for the same time every day. But now you have a choice. Hit the gym or skip? Over time, your choice to follow the path of least resistance is adding up. You notice you're drifting in your overall health and strength.

You're suffering from the lack of structure, and you've chosen to drink more to ease the pain as you drift through life. Thinking some alcohol will calm things down for you, you only develop a new dependency to find temporary peace and cope with the symptoms from drifting in your fitness. Now you are reliant on alcohol to give you peace, and your spouse is getting more irritated with you because you're falling apart and not helping out around the house. Dishes are piling up, the house is falling apart, and they've had it. You feel like you are easily irritated, and most of the time, you take this out on the people closest to you. You don't even like yourself, but you don't know how to change. Over time, your marriage is destroyed since you've ignored your spouse and retreated to the "man cave" or "she shed" to hide from the stress.

Now, your divorce is final, your kids don't want to be around you, and you never discovered the bigger mission for your life. All because you avoided working out and chose to drink to deal with the symptoms of loss of mission and identity. We must see that everything we do or avoid doing is connected. It might sound like I'm exaggerating this point, but this happens all the time. People are falling apart because they are escaping and retreating. It's time for mission-minded leaders like you to deal with their hearts and lead their homes the right way.

Intentional Action

Fourth, *each corrective action should be smooth, coordinated, and intentional.* We must be deliberate. Do you know anyone who is all in with everything they do? One day, they're just maxing out their schedule with a new business they started. Then as time goes by, they have a new passion to dedicate their life to. A few months later, they think running is the coolest thing ever, so they begin to train for a race. Before the race, they realize they really want to be an author, so they begin to write a book. They stop running and preparing for the race because the book is taking up all their time.

All-in, all the time. Do you know anyone who is like that? Until they correct it, that person is never going to develop momentum in their life since their course is constantly changing. There is no smooth, coordinated, corrective action. Just because something becomes a person's new passion doesn't mean they have to commit all their time and energy to that activity. You don't get from Colorado to Hawaii by consistently rerouting and changing the flight plan. That's how you run out of fuel and crash. Deception loves to draw your focus by manipulating your motives, causing you to overcorrect and overcommit.

> **DECEPTION LOVES TO DRAW YOUR FOCUS BY MANIPULATING YOUR MOTIVES, CAUSING YOU TO OVERCORRECT AND OVERCOMMIT.**

WHAT ARE YOUR INSTRUMENTS?

I'm sure that by now, you are saying, "I need an instrument panel, but I have no idea where to start." That's exactly why I'm here. I got you. There are many instruments in an aircraft cockpit. The six instruments you heard me reference in the opening example were a combination of my preferences and the primary instruments that would tell me the truth about my aircraft's current position. I'm going to provide you with the primary instruments for just about anybody's life: peace, people, purpose, and power—which, you will notice, are in exact opposition to the weapons of mass deception.

Once you've chosen your instruments, you'll determine your scan frequency. Every pilot has their own "primary scan." This is the order that their eyes follow when they check their flight instruments. Your scan has a tempo, a pace, and a rhythm. As you implement your scan more often, you'll begin to increase the pace and thereby increase your ability to catch a deviation from your original intention sooner, resulting in creating a positive pattern in your life. Author James

Clear, in his book *Atomic Habits,* talks about a concept called "Avoid the Second Mistake." He says:

> *According to a study published in the* European Journal of Social Psychology, *missing any single day of a particular habit has no impact on your long-term ability to stick to the habit. It doesn't matter when it occurs, making a mistake and slipping up does not alter the long-term outcome . . . if you find a way to get back on track.*
>
> *Furthermore, top performers in all fields make mistakes all the time. Athletes skip workouts. CEOs forget to meditate. Nutritionists eat unhealthy meals. Artists loaf around in bed all day and ignore their craft. These people are human, just like you and me. There are many points during their careers when they make a mistake, skip a session, and approach their tasks with the enthusiasm of a sleep-deprived manatee.*
>
> *What separates the elite performers from everyone else? Not perfection, but consistency. This is why the most important thing is not to prevent mistakes altogether, but to avoid making a mistake twice in a row. Errors are part of the process, but they shouldn't become part of the pattern.*
>
> *One mistake is just an outlier. Two mistakes is the beginning of a pattern. Killing this pattern before it snowballs into something bigger is one reason why learning how to get back on track quickly is an essential skill for building good habits.*[31]

As the weeks progress, you'll notice your instruments changing based on your circumstances, but over time, you'll begin to catch the deviations quicker, avoid the second mistake, and adjust as needed. For now, just start by checking your instruments once a week. Just pick a date and time, and take five minutes to scan your progress

---

31 James Clear, "Avoid the Second Mistake," *James Clear,* 25 June 2019, https://jamesclear.com/second-mistake.

display panel (PDP). Applying the *4-I Instrument Framework* will help you determine which gauges you want on your PDP and in which order you want to scan them.

My personal PDP includes the gauges for what I value most in my life: peace, people, purpose, and power. They all start with "P," but that is coincidental. I asked myself the four "I" questions below to determine what I value most at this time in my life, how I would recognize a deviation, and how I would adjust to maximize their impact. And remember: it is not uncommon for the instruments on your PDP to change according to different seasons of life. Start with what you need now, and feel free to adjust as necessary. I'll lead you through it.

PROGRESS DISPLAY PANEL

4-I INSTRUMENT FRAMEWORK

As you review your progress display panel, it's critical to understand that every instrument has its own importance, indicators to watch for, instructions for applying corrections, and insights that can be learned from the situation. When we apply the 4-I Instrument Framework to our lives, we maximize the lessons learned and our intended results.

Here are some quick questions to get you started:

Importance: *Why does this instrument gauge matter to me?*

Indicators: *What signals will show my current status and path?*

Instruction: *What corrections should I make? (We'll talk about this more in phase 4.)*

Insight: *What deeper understanding can come from this?*

The best teacher is not experience; it's *evaluated* experience. When we take time to gather insight from what we observed on our PDP, we will become more effective and resilient leaders.

> THE BEST TEACHER IS NOT EXPERIENCE; IT'S EVALUATED EXPERIENCE. WHEN WE TAKE TIME TO GATHER INSIGHT, WE WILL BECOME MORE EFFECTIVE AND RESILIENT LEADERS.

PEACE INSTRUMENT GAUGE

Peace is in direct opposition to the first weapon of mass deception, the pressure of performance. Because it is so important (the first I in the 4-I Instrument Framework), I use it as the ultimate instrument for my life. This is that stress-free, calm confidence that we all want to experience more often.

When I feel pressure (the *indicator*), I purposefully shift my mind into a state of peace. How? I mentally disconnect from the situation, observe what's really happening, decide what needs to change, and then jump back in with focus. In other words, when I begin to hurry and rush through life, feeling more depleted as the day goes on, I detect the onset of that deception by reminding myself that this is not a natural emotional state that I need to maintain. Instead of pressure being a trigger for anger, it's a trigger for me to consciously disconnect for a moment, observe the situation, choose an appropriate response, and then reengage with intentionality.

After my awareness shifts to realize that the pressure of performance is trying to infiltrate, I can apply practical adjustments to my life right away. What works for me is to quicken my situational awareness to look at the big picture and remind myself that Jesus stated His peace is with us. So I remind myself that I don't need to generate an emotion of peace. Instead, I simply need to remove pressure because the peace is already there.

Speaking of pressure, a few months ago, I spoke to a baseball team and asked them the question, "How many here feel like they are behind in life? How many of you feel like no matter what you do, it's never enough?" I couldn't believe it. About 90 percent had their hands up. How about you? What does your peace instrument gauge say about your life? Are you losing a sense of peace because you also feel behind?

When my peace instrument gauge indicates a decline, the first *instruction* (the third "I") to implement is a shift in my focus. I mentally detach from the situation, and I shift my focus to other people. When I discovered that fear falls when we focus on others, it changed everything. Whenever I felt frustrated, anxious, stressed, tense, exhausted, and run-down (FASTER) for a long period of time, I would shift my focus, and everything would become clear again.

FEAR FALLS WHEN WE FOCUS ON OTHERS.

If your peace gauge is showing a decline, remember that Jesus says His yoke is easy, and His burden is light (Matthew 11:30). Correcting your state of peace is not about striving or forcing yourself to follow religious, man-made rules. In fact, that often steals your peace and places pressure right back on your shoulders.

In a season of my life when the weapons hit hard, God reminded me through multiple people who said, "Adam, I think God just wants you to seek His kingdom first, and everything else will be taken care of." When I first heard this, I was blown away. *How is that possibly good advice? What a simple approach to a complex life!*

But nonetheless, I chose to trust, and I'm glad I did. I believe if we simply trust God and we set our intentions to seek His peace, He'll take care of the rest. But we need to trust our instruments.

PEOPLE INSTRUMENT GAUGE

Israel McGuicken, the man who called out my drift in chapter 7, taught me that relationships are a leader's greatest currency. How are yours looking? Mine were hurting—not just my marriage but neighbors, family, friends, business partners . . . all were pretty rough. When you place a consistent focus on the status of your relationships, it will help you respond to the stealth attack of the second weapon of mass deception, the altar of impact, before it becomes destructive.

Many people think the altar of impact only relates to their family, but in reality, no relationship is safe. We can sacrifice relationships with friends, mentors, team members, and even acquaintances on the altar of impact. If you consistently focus on who's next, how are you caring for who's now?

When correcting drift, the first instrument we need to watch and adjust is the peace gauge which correlates with the second gauge on the PDP: people. Here's why. If you can only give what you have, then what happens if you don't have peace? How will you give peace, calm confidence, and assurance to others if you are living in chaos? Why would people want to follow you if you aren't enjoyable to be around? Just a thought.

If relationships are a leader's greatest currency, how often do we miss an opportunity to deepen a current relationship in pursuit of the next one?

> **IF RELATIONSHIPS ARE A LEADER'S GREATEST CURRENCY, HOW OFTEN DO WE MISS AN OPPORTUNITY TO DEEPEN A CURRENT RELATIONSHIP IN PURSUIT OF THE NEXT ONE?**

Here's my belief. God assigned you a family. If God assigns you something, He will also give you the grace needed to complete the assignment. I had no idea *how* my marriage was going to improve (and it needed to because my people gauge indicated deviation), but I knew that God's supernatural power could take care of it. I believe, for most of us, our marriage (if you're married) is an assignment from

God, meaning, if He gave you a spouse and children, they are your assignment—not just an obligation. These people are part of your purpose, and you are part of theirs. God will empower you in your areas of weakness as you lead them. If you feel disconnected from them (an indicator), it doesn't need to stay this way. If you've never seen a great marriage in action, you are not limited by the examples you have seen. You don't have to have a marriage that follows the war-torn path of your parents.

I am convinced that your family is a key component of your purpose on earth. However, it's not only that. It's not just about you. What if your family needs you to step up and engage with intentionality because you are preparing *them* for *their* greater callings and assignments?

And what about friends, employees, neighbors, and coworkers? You might find yourself never being able to make time for some of your good friends because you're always on the move, focused on building your network. They might need you, but you don't notice it because you always have the blinders on. Here's what I know: I hurt a lot of relationships because of my addiction to achievement and constant desire to impact people I'd never met before. I didn't realize that the people already in my life were the ones I had the greatest opportunity to impact. My relationships were a revolving door, and that wasn't fair to them.

One of my most significant life changes occurred after I scanned my PDP and saw imminent danger indicated by my people gauge. In that moment, I felt like people were sent from all around the world to help me recover from my loss of identity. Joshua, a business owner who sells premium wallets, told me about a calling to business. David and Margo taught me how to break free of religious mindsets and connect with a deeper version of the best version of myself. Israel and Rebecca pulled me out of my pit of destruction and began to show me how to simply enjoy life with my family and with God. Richard and Chasity showed me the value of one thoughtful investment.

I found a connection to a community of people who shared my values but who didn't value me for my performance. They wanted to spend time with me because they believed in the value of people. Look for people whom you can live life with. They will help improve your ability to lead and love your own family.

As I began to correct this part of my life, everything started to come together. I began to see that family was not just an obligation but an assignment. Trust your instruments.

PURPOSE INSTRUMENT GAUGE

The purpose instrument gauge is one we cannot afford to neglect because usually, our confidence and clarity are tied to it. When you realize that you are positioned for purpose, everything changes. When you begin to see that you were intentionally designed to be short instead of tall (or vice versa) for a reason greater than your current circumstance, everything changes. When you see that you were created to be strong instead of intellectual (or vice versa) for a reason, everything changes.

It will all begin to make sense when you can see the purpose of you. When you see that you have personality traits, characteristics, skills, experiences, and a particular lens through which you see the world for a reason, you'll never want to compare yourself to another person again. When you don't see these things, your purpose gauge plummets or spins out of control, indicating that you are vulnerable to the weapons of mass deception.

If we want to detect and dismantle the cycle of comparison in our lives, then I think we need to understand that every one of us has a different purpose for our life. There will be deep commonalities, but besides stepping up and leading where you are called to lead, I think you will find that there are unique areas of life in which you are meant to be successful and others that you are meant to avoid. There are people that only you can reach, and realizing this can bring tremendous purpose to your life. I hope to bring an impact to your life through this book, but I also hope you will pay it forward.

I'm a speaker and leadership tactician. I train leaders to become more influential, effective, and resilient. I don't teach data analysis. I don't teach how to cook. I don't teach you how to work on your car. I don't help people with their finances. Why? Because that's not my lane. I don't hold the key to unlock those areas of life. However, if you have a leadership gap in your organization, your leaders are maxed out, your people are leaving, and morale is suffering, I can help. Maxed-out leaders can become transformational leaders who are free to operate in alignment with who they are and what they represent.

Sadly, one thing I find often is that many people are searching for their purpose and possibly will never find it. I think this is because they are searching outside for affirmation instead of inside for answers. As Trent Shelton says, "You are purpose.... Your life is purpose."[32] I found that when I received the proper image of who God was demonstrated through the life of Jesus—kind, loving, inclusive, and peaceful—I began to reflect the proper image of who I was.

Here's something I live by: *proper positioning produces permanent confidence.*

When I am properly positioned, based on who I am and what I bring to the table, I'm naturally confident. It's the same for you. It's

---

[32] "How to Find Your Purpose | Trent Shelton." *YouTube*, 27 Dec. 2020, https://www.youtube.com/watch?v=y1ngPxYcDNs.

not faking it until you make it. It's understanding that you are where you are meant to be, and out of that, solutions can flow to others. Your purpose gauge will stay in a safe range.

I believe your life is filled with purpose. Everything is connected. Your purpose is not just your career but much larger. The mission is not just your job but a greater, more expansive view of your life.

A few months ago before a speaking engagement, my wife looked over at me and smiled. She said, "I'm so proud of you. This is truly your purpose."

As I looked back over to her while I was playing with our girls on the playground, I said, "You're right. It is my purpose, but so are you, so are our girls, and so is my business." I realized that, despite our circumstances, I could always find purpose.

I remember realizing how important my purpose was to recognizing my role as the father of my two girls. I realized who I am, and what I bring to the table is intentionality, love, and leadership. For a while, I wished I were more fun, carefree, and organized. But then I realized that's not who I am, and that's not who I need to be. (Did you catch that?)

My family already has a nurturing person. My family already has someone who can bring a carefree, easygoing attitude to the atmosphere. My girls already have a mom who loves to plan and organize every microdetail of life. Thank God, or I don't know where we would be. I'm the kind of guy who grabs two pieces of bread and some meat from the fridge and eats them separately instead of taking the extra step to make a sandwich. My wife is the kind of lady who takes those, combines them, adds all the fancy condiments, and toasts the sandwich. She complements me perfectly!

Our girls are already getting the traits that I don't possess from other family members. My job is to use what God has placed inside of me to work alongside other family members and our friends to shape our girls into who they were called to be. This is the difference between the danger of uniformity and the power of unity. We aren't all trying to be the same, but we are embracing and leveraging our differences.

You don't need to be anyone you're not, but you do need to be the best version of who you've always been. Then, bring that to the table unapologetically. Once you understand that, you'll begin to appreciate others for what they bring to the table instead of feeling like you need to be more like they are.

> YOU DON'T NEED TO BE ANYONE YOU'RE NOT, BUT YOU DO NEED TO BE THE BEST VERSION OF WHO YOU'VE ALWAYS BEEN.

When you understand your purpose and unique design, it's time to look at ways you can add value to the people around you. Repair broken relationships by closing the gap. Be the first person to step up and say you messed up, you forgot to keep in touch, you let things fall off your radar, and you don't want that anymore. Watch how people will respond when you take that step. I bet you that the greatest relationships of your life are ahead of you.

Trust your instruments.

POWER INSTRUMENT GAUGE

Okay, who doesn't want to have more power, energy, and strength? Well, despite how much you want to have, is it possible this is an area in which you've been hurting the most?

After speaking to thousands of high-performance leaders, I found that a lot of people lose their power when they lose their title. They lose their power when they lose their position. They allow the limitation of a label to determine not only who they are but who they can become.

For instance, if you are reading low on the power instrument gauge, it's possible you feel like you are maxed out and weighed down or even drifting through life, holding back who you really are. I'll never forget the moment when I realized that my power was fading. I was ordering a meal and realized that when people spoke to me, I broke eye contact. I would glance away and change my tone. For some reason, I didn't have the confidence to look back at someone else with strength. The same thing would happen when people asked me questions like, "What do you do?" Once I caught myself, I realized I was doing it everywhere with everyone. I was ashamed of who I was and how my life was progressing, and because of that, my power was dropping.

You, too, might notice your self-image and confidence have been declining.

The trap of title hates it when you recognize that your power doesn't come from your position but your presence. See, I am convinced there is power in your presence, but what about you? This realization stops you from overthinking and underselling yourself based on whatever man-made measurement or qualifier has been placed on you because you realize the solutions are already inside of you. To release them to others, all you need to do is show up.

This is the power in our presence. When we show up, God shows up with us. We are not alone. We are empowered. This is when we stop saying things like, "I was just a truck driver," "I only have my associate's degree," "I'm only a lieutenant," "I was only in the Reserves," "I'm only a director," "I'm only a stay-at-home mom," or "When I'm a vice president, then I can. . . ." Not plugging in to the power of your presence creates a perpetual cycle that is stealing the joy right out of you.

NOT PLUGGING IN TO THE POWER OF YOUR PRESENCE CREATES A PERPETUAL CYCLE THAT IS STEALING THE JOY RIGHT OUT OF YOU.

It's never enough because we don't allow it to be enough.

We don't need to entertain this idea anymore. We aren't *just* humans. We are God's greatest creation, and we aren't living with the consequences of the first people's decision anymore. Instead, we are living as redeemed people—the new creation that no one ever experienced before—when we accept Christ into our lives. He made mankind and said this is VERY good. God loves mankind so much that He became one of us. Through the cross, He restored everything we ever lost. You'll never unlock your power if you don't realize how valuable you are. If you don't realize the power that lives inside of you as a high-performance man or woman, then you are consistently going to miss the opportunities right in front of you.

Trust your instruments.

SUMMARY

As we close this chapter, please do not neglect the Four Keys to Correction. Write them down. Share them with others. Find someone to call out your drift. Also, remember this: Deception is not always about getting you to do the wrong thing. Sometimes, it's the right thing in the wrong order. My intention is not to preach to you but just to share what worked for me. I'm not speaking from education but experience. You don't need to believe what I believe in order for me to be in your corner. I'm here for you regardless.

Your motives to serve and change the world amaze me. They are admirable. That's why I took a year to write this book. I want us to succeed, but in order to do this in a way that is sustainable, we need to define, detect, and dismantle the weapons with relentless determination and focus.

CHAPTER 14

BREAK THE KILL CHAIN

"On March 28, 1979, a sightseeing flight crashed into a mountain in Antarctica, killing all of the 279 people onboard. An investigation determined that the crew had not been informed of a two-degree correction made to the plane's flight path the night before, causing the plane's navigation system to route them toward Mount Erebus instead of through McMurdo Sound. Two degrees doesn't sound like a lot, but in aviation terms, even one degree is huge. That's why pilots are taught the 1 in 60 rule, which states that after 60 miles a one-degree error in heading will result in straying off course by one mile."[33] That is the significance of the slightest deviation magnified over a period of time. At first, it can seem insignificant, but the greater the distance, the harder it is to get back on course.

---
33 Jeff Haden, "The 1 in 60 Rule: How Remarkably Successful People Stay on Track to . . ." *Inc.*, https://www.inc.com/jeff-haden/the-1-in-60-rule-how-remarkably-successful-people-stay-on-track-to-accomplish-their-biggest-goals.html.

When beginning to defeat the weapons of mass deception that were hidden in my heart, I learned that the easiest way to destroy them was not through additional effort but complete awareness. By bringing what was hidden into the light, I was able to dismantle the weapon. Hidden mechanisms were revealed and removed.

I began by having simple conversations with people who led me to find the answers to my deepest questions. The first year, the most important question these people helped me embrace was simply, Why? Constantly being asked by others why I thought something and where that thought might've originated helped me break through limiting beliefs. And while talking was helpful, this analysis was most effective when I physically "mapped" my thought processes—either using paper and pencil or an online graphic organizing tool.

I began to see correlations between the pain I was feeling and the thoughts I was thinking. I started to see that most of my problems had one thing in common—me. And I knew from experience as an entrepreneur that there were only a few things that I could really control: my thoughts, attitudes, and actions. It seemed that behind every area of adversity, there was an advancement awaiting me. A new level. A new way to operate.

It became clear that there were results in my life that I did not want and actions I could take to create the life I originally imagined. So first, I cleared the distractions. I simplified as much as possible so that I could focus on rediscovering the connection to my most valued relationships. If you are happy with the state of your life, then keep doing what you're doing. But if you're like me, and you know that something needs to change, keep reading.

I had to look at the patterns in my thoughts and the various ways that I was triggered. Then, I had to analyze them to see where I could change. I didn't pursue research-driven education in a scientific field, but others have, and their findings validate what I was experiencing. Dr. Caroline Leaf, a cognitive neuroscientist, explains that when a toxic thought stays in the darkness, it cannot be changed, but when that toxic thought is brought into the light, it becomes malleable.[34] Then, it can be changed. The strength of a toxic thought comes from the fact that it is hiding in the complexities of your neural processing. A weapon of mass deception is similar. The weapon's greatest strength lies in its secrecy. Just like the development of toxic thoughts, a weapon of mass deception becomes evident by observing patterns in your life.

After defining the weapon and detecting the deception, it is time to disrupt its pattern. This is when you fight back with everything you have. You take a stand for your family, your relationships, and your purpose. When you disrupt the pattern thereby dismantling the weapon, you step into the greatest phase of freedom. And it all becomes practical through a concept I call Breaking the Kill Chain. It's a concept that was taught to me as an Army Black Hawk pilot, but today I am teaching it to you as a fellow leader who wants to see you recover from this attack and become stronger than ever. This concept can be life-changing, and I hope it serves you. Considering I have zero claims of expertise or education in this area, I'm going to reference the experts in the industry—in our case, Dr. Leaf.

Despite popular belief, neuroscientific research continues to support the idea that we don't deal with a toxic thought by simply burying it with new words. Instead, it all ties back to belief. Dr. Leaf explains that when we say words that we don't believe—a practice referred to as cognitive dissonance—we actually cause brain damage.[35] I don't know

---

[34] Dr. Caroline Leaf, "How to Make Intrusive Thoughts Work for You, Not against You," *Dr. Leaf*, 10 Oct. 2022, https://drleaf.com/blogs/news/how-to-make-intrusive-thoughts-work-for-you-not-against-you.
[35] Ed Mylett, "Heal Your Mind and Control Your Brain—An Interview with Dr. Caroline Leaf," 30 Mar. 2021, 46:25, *YouTube*, https://www.youtube.com/watch?v=MwvctN3Uejg.

about you, but that shocked me. To discover that I could damage my brain if I consistently say things I don't believe caused me to really become careful about aligning my words to my beliefs—and changing my beliefs if they don't serve others and myself.

Dr. Leaf also explains that we are not a victim of our biology, formation, and experiences.[36] Instead, she emphasizes that we can change our brain if we apply laser focus to an area of our life. To me, this means you aren't stuck thinking toxic thoughts. Great news, right?

WEAPONS OF MASS DECEPTION MIGHT BE POWERFUL, BUT THEY ARE ALSO FRAGILE.

These first few principles helped me realize that weapons of mass deception might be powerful, but they are also fragile.

Dr. Leaf explains:

We can never rid ourselves of all pain or suffering. However, we can learn how to reconceptualize what has happened to us, which is to view a memory from a new perspective so we no longer feel overwhelmed or trapped when we think about something that previously caused us emotional distress.[37]

By implementing the practices of mapping out and breaking the kill chain, I was able to analyze a series of thoughts, triggers, and experiences and view them with a new perspective.

---

[36] Dr. Caroline Leaf, "You Are Not a Victim of Your Biology!" *Dr. Leaf*, 3 Oct. 2018, https://drleaf.com/blogs/news/you-are-not-a-victim-of-your-biology?_pos=1&_sid=b55e714a4&_ss=r.
[37] Dr. Caroline Leaf, "Neuroplasticity: What It Is & How to Harness Its Power for Your Benefit," *Dr. Leaf*, 10 Apr. 2022, https://drleaf.com/blogs/news/neuroplasticity-what-it-is-how-to-harness-its-power-for-your-benefit.

THE HIDDEN PATTERN OF THE WEAPON

The term kill chain was introduced to me as a military concept related to the structure of an attack. The military describes it as a structured attack often consisting of the following: target identification, force dispatch to target, decision and order to attack the target, and finally, the *destruction of the target.*[38]

In simple terms, the kill chain is a series of steps that have to take place in order to destroy a target. So if a target is not identified, obviously, the target cannot be destroyed. Additionally, if there isn't a decision made to attack a target, the target cannot be destroyed. These microdetails have to happen in order for a target to be destroyed. In my case, this applied to the aircraft. Instead of evading a missile after it's already been fired, they taught us to first focus on defeating the person who has to fire it.

Not only that, but if someone can stop the supply of ammunition from getting to the rocket launcher, then the enemy won't have anything to shoot us with. This is another way to break the same kill chain. Every kill chain is slightly different based on a weapon's capabilities and limitations. The true power of leveraging a kill chain comes from being able to see and study the structure of a possible attack in order to exploit its weak points. If you see it, you can defeat it.

I found that the same thing can help us visualize and defeat a weapon of mass deception. If we can see the pattern, we can defeat its power. By simply seeing the connections between various thoughts, triggers, and experiences, we can begin to plan a new way of responding to similar situations.

---

38 BalaGanesh, "SOC Interview Questions and Answers – Cyber Security Analyst - Security Investigation," *Security Investigation - Be the First to Investigate,* 24 Dec. 2021, https://www.socinvestigation.com/soc-interview-questions-and-answers-cyber-security-analyst/.

IF YOU SEE THE ATTACK COMING, YOU CAN DEFEAT IT.

I've narrowed down the essential elements for a weapons of mass deception kill chain into five simple steps. If you map out the complexities of your entire life, you will certainly see more, but for the purpose of understanding this concept, we will stick with these five essential steps.

THE KILL CHAIN SIMPLIFIED

Nearly every weapon of mass deception follows this kill chain:

1) FIELDS OF FORMATION shape a person's language, perception, and mindset.
2) CRITICAL EXPERIENCES conflict, confirm, or challenge a belief taught during formation.
3) PASSIVE INTERPRETATIONS occur without someone noticing that their mind has rapidly sorted and assigned meaning to an experience.
4) AUTOMATED ACTIONS subconsciously begin to guide behavior as the person repeatedly and unknowingly allows a hidden deception to lead them.
5) REINFORCED RESULTS change a person's environment and beliefs, bringing widespread damage over a period of time.

Those five steps are all you need to remember. Let's look at how this simple framework can help you recognize destructive patterns and plan your responses from this point forward. Once you start to use this, it will quickly become natural for you to defeat future onsets of the weapon.

Weapons of Mass Deception Kill Chain

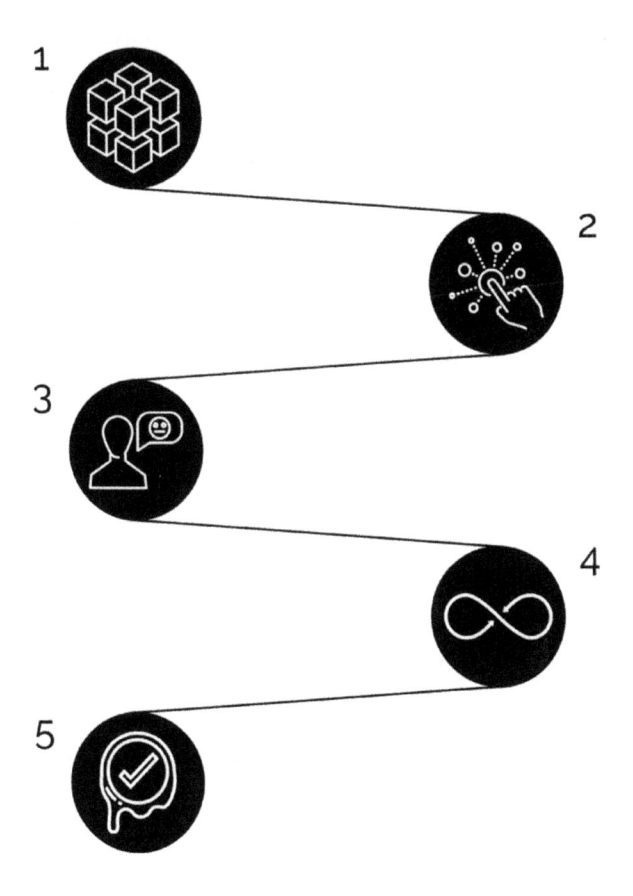

1
2
3
4
5

THE "5 STEPS TO DISMANTLING A KILL CHAIN" FRAMEWORK

Let's break down each critical step in the kill chain using the expertise of our go-to resource for this chapter: cognitive neuroscientist Dr. Caroline Leaf.

1) Fields of Formation

Our fields of formation influence our perception of "normal." We are constantly formed by people, places, tribes, cultures, social norms, and many other elements. This formation plants a seed in the center of the human experience that grows over time: communication, values, self-worth, and many other aspects of life are influenced by this.

The culture of the military was a strong field of formation in my life. It played a major role in the way I communicated and operated both in and out of uniform. Starting at twelve years old, I was in a military uniform through the Civil Air Patrol. At eighteen years old, I joined the Army. During the most formative years of my life, I was shaped by a mission mindset in a high-stakes culture. This field of formation taught me to be intentional, disciplined, and structured but also conflicted with the way other people around me were living their lives. It was at those times that I had to assess if what was forming me was productive for helping me develop into who I needed to become.

2) Critical Experiences

Throughout life, we encounter critical experiences that often *confirm, conflict,* or *challenge* what we've learned from a field of formation. If you recall what we discussed in phase 1 about the origins of the weapons, some of these experiences can be tied to transition, training, trauma, and timing. Dr. Leaf differentiates between big events that impact us in dramatic and unforeseen ways and situations we deal with every day that, over time, impact physical and emotional health.[39] These experiences might seem insignificant at first, but I'll admit that even if an event seemed "minor," there were quite a few that I would replay in my mind that caused me to lose my sense of peace and power.

Transitioning out of the military was a critical experience that I wasn't prepared for. I thought life after the service would be smooth sailing. I didn't realize I would dwell on my lack of deployment or the fact that I couldn't fly anymore. It was like the main adventure of my life had ended. Today, I see things from an entirely new perspective, but back then, I felt like I was dying inside, and I wasn't even thirty.

3) Passive Interpretations

After we encounter a critical experience, our subconscious mind is forced to quickly process how to interpret the event. It's heavily

---

39 Dr. Caroline Leaf, "How to Heal from Trauma, Signs of Secondary Trauma, and How EMDR Can Help with Trauma Recovery and PTSD with Therapist and Trauma Expert Alyssa Mancao," *Dr. Leaf,* https://drleaf.com/blogs/news/how-to-heal-from-trauma-signs-of-secondary-trauma-and-how-emdr-can-help-with-trauma-recovery-and-ptsd-with-therapist-and-trauma-expert-alyssa-mancao?_pos=1&_sid=a1ab12dc6&_ss=r.

influenced by our fields of formation, internalized, and applied through a basic survive and thrive response. Without knowing the truth, this is where we are often introduced to a thought planted in the core of a weapon of mass deception. And, while I mentioned a critical experience, "everything that you experience leaves its mark on your brain."[40]

I think this was the stage when I really started to feel like an outsider. I told myself that other people didn't get me, appreciate me, or know who I really was. I started to see people differently and just wanted to run away. Without a uniform and title, I didn't have a path. I didn't know how to live, but it was "obvious" people didn't get me. The truth, today, is that it wasn't them; it was me. I didn't get me. I didn't know how to see myself as more than a pilot. Whenever I told people I used to fly, people thought it was awesome, and they seemed to appreciate me differently. I didn't think people would like the real Adam, but I also wasn't going to give them a chance to decide for themselves.

4) Automated Actions

Once these passive interpretations are sorted out and locked into our subconscious, our body follows. We basically move back into autopilot mode with these quick decisions and new meanings guiding our future actions. When being led by a weapon of mass deception, we begin to practice false beliefs unknowingly allowing them to grow into our *core* beliefs.

---

[40] "How Experience Shapes the Brain," *ELife*, ELife Sciences Publications, Ltd, 17 Mar. 2020, https://elifesciences.org/digests/52743/how-experience-shapes-the-brain.

At this step, I like to think that the weapon moves from the "head to the heart." The more action we take the more our beliefs are normalized. Dr. Leaf explains, "95% of our day is driven by automatized drivers. When we know how to change our mind, we rewire neural networks in the brain that create useful, sustainable, and automatized actions and attitudes."[41]

5) Reinforced Results

The compounded effect of our actions can create a world that we don't want to live in. It can feel like there is no way out. This final stage is similar to when the weapon destroys the target. I found, in my own life, that once I was running with a limiting belief on autopilot, the results started to stack up pretty quickly. First, I didn't like my work conditions. Then, I didn't feel a connection with the people closest to me. Finally, I began to feel frustrated with and ashamed of myself. I didn't even want to look at the man in the mirror because he was an embarrassment.

Dr. Leaf concludes:

The more exposure we have to whatever is going on in our lives, the stronger the encoding becomes and the more power and energy the resultant thought (or encoded neural network) gets. What this essentially means is that whatever we think about the most grows. Thoughts are the drivers behind how we think, feel and choose, which, in turn, generates what we say and do, and how we see life.[42]

---

41 Dr. Caroline Leaf, "Neuroplasticity: What It Is & How to Harness Its Power for Your Benefit," *Dr. Leaf*, 10 Apr. 2022, https://drleaf.com/blogs/news/neuroplasticity-what-it-is-how-to-harness-its-power-for-your-benefit.
42 Dr. Caroline Leaf, "How to Use Mind-Management to Rewrite & Redefine Your Life Story," *Dr. Leaf*, 10 Apr. 2022, https://drleaf.com/blogs/news/how-to-use-mind-management-to-rewrite-redefine-your-life-story.

Once the entire kill chain is mapped out, you can begin to break it through different means. Once I recognized what triggered me, I could change those things. Other times, I avoided situations that were not beneficial to me. For instance, anytime I had to work on excel reports, I felt stressed which caused me to act like an ass (I'm talking about the donkey, of course). I couldn't change the fact that my job required me to turn in reports. But I did see some options to help limit my ass-likeness.

> I could stop, breathe, and create a state of peace in and around me for that moment.
> I could study how to improve in this area and become more skilled in making spreadsheets.
> I could give that task to someone else.
> I could just leave this type of job. Maybe it's not aligned with my unique design and gifts.

Regardless of which way I chose to break my kill chain, once I saw it, I could defeat it.

EXAMPLES OF THE KILL CHAIN

Before we dive into the specifics of each weapon and its kill chain, let's just take a moment to look at two scenarios.

Scenario 1: Just Like Your Father

Fifteen-year-old Tyson Brown is growing up in the Queensbridge housing projects, spending most of his time with his overworked mom, two friends from the neighborhood, and school. One day, Tyson is arrested for armed robbery. Growing up, whenever Tyson would get in trouble, his mom would say, "You're just like your father." Tyson has never met his father, a gang member known for armed robberies and assaults, who is currently behind bars. In the back of his mind, Tyson thinks to himself, *She is right. I'm just like my father.* The weapon has led him down a continued path of violence and crime. His mom is run-down and can't bear to watch as her son follows the path of his father.

> - Fields of Formation: Mom, neighborhood, friends
> - Critical Experiences: Arrested for stealing.
> - Passive Interpretations: *Mom was right. I'm just like my father.*
> - Automated Actions: Continues to steal and fight in school.
> - Reinforced Results: Eventually, he is incarcerated just like his dad.

Scenario 2: I'll Never Leave You

Thirteen-year-old Mary Jameson lives with a loving and supportive family. Mary leaves her backpack at school one day and asks her mom to go back and pick it up. Mary experiences a tragedy when her mother is killed in a car crash on her way to school. Her mother always said she would never leave Mary, but now she's gone. A weapon of mass deception causes her to believe that the crash is her fault because if she hadn't left her bookbag at school, her mom wouldn't have been on the road, and she never would have crashed. Mary begins to hide from the world. She avoids people and is filled with guilt for something the weapon is causing her to believe she did. She feels like an outsider, not knowing the weapon is keeping her trapped in the past. She sticks to herself because she doesn't want to hurt anyone else.

> - Fields of Formation: Family, school, sports
> - Critical Experiences: Mother is killed in a car crash.
> - Passive Interpretations: *It's my fault.*
> - Automated Actions: Mary avoids people and keeps to herself.

> Reinforced Results: Two years later, Mary is lost. She has pushed everyone away and has no one left to trust.

WHO DO YOU SAY I AM?

When I started dismantling the weapons through a series of questions, I didn't realize everything that I'm explaining to you about the kill chain and actually disrupting these patterns. It took time, but eventually, I discovered all of my weapons were reinforced—and it didn't matter whom I was with—by one toxic thought: *Who do YOU say I am?* I was convinced that if I achieved more, I would become more, and *you* and everyone else would see me as more.

I didn't really know who I was or what I was created to do. I wanted other people to tell me. We see the same thing happened with Jesus, but He handled it the right way. In Matthew 16, Luke 9, and Mark 8, Jesus asked Peter two questions: "Who do they say I am?" and "Who do you say I am?" But here's the key: Jesus didn't change how He felt about Himself based on how Peter or anyone else answered the questions. Instead, He knew who He was because He allowed the Father to tell Him. He did not change how He saw Himself based on how others saw Him. He didn't say, "You know what? You're right. I didn't see it at first, but I am a carpenter." That's what the trap of title would have done. Instead, He knew He was more than His position or what others saw.

For me, that was not the case. Based on my toxic thought patterns, I constantly changed for other people in order to feel appreciated. I always brought my A game because I wanted to impress and perform. I did all of this not only to belong but to hear from other people who they thought or said I was. I think my deeper subconscious desire, probably my passive interpretation, was thinking, *If I hear it from people I respect, then maybe I'll believe it myself.*

Here's what I know today: as long as I looked to the wrong field of formation for my identity, it would never give me the results of confidence and clarity that I was desperately desiring.

Even as an Army National Guard company commander, that is what I believed. It didn't go away as I climbed through the ranks because the kill chain was still active. As my influence grew greater, the weapons grew stronger. The pressure of performance connected to the trap of title was evidenced by the sacrifice of every meaningful relationship in my life on the altar of impact. It was a three-pronged attack against my life and my family, and I couldn't see it. When I acknowledged the indicators of each weapon, it became clear. I was stressed, discouraged, exhausted, tense, and on edge, and my family was irritated. The weapons were present. I just couldn't see them for what they were. I didn't need to treat the symptoms. I needed to BREAK THE KILL CHAIN.

WHAT'S YOUR KILL CHAIN?

What might your primary kill chain be—not just the kill chain for the four weapons but the kill chain causing most of your pain? What pathway—fields of formation, critical experiences, passive interpretations, automated actions, and reinforced results—causes you to see the worst side of yourself when it actually matters the most? What might that kill chain look like?

When you conducted the battle damage assessment, you learned what weapon has been affecting you the most. Take a moment to map out how you think this weapon has been hurting you. Give it a shot. You might want to work backward, starting with the result that you have but that you don't want to have anymore. What influences, experiences, and triggers are connected to this kill chain?

Here's an easy example: You're overweight. You don't want to be overweight. What automated actions have caused this? Maybe you eat when you're bored. What interpretations and experiences might have led to this type of eating? Maybe it's that you feel food makes you feel complete. What formations taught you this? Maybe you have a family of heavy eaters. Now that you can see the kill chain, what can you do about it? You can schedule your meals or plan what you're going to eat on a given day. You can decide, from now on, that when you feel bored, you'll go for a walk. Just like that, the rest of the kill chain is broken.

You can't change your original field of formation, but you can change your interpretation of the critical events in your life. You can also add new fields of formation to help you going forward. Maybe you join a fitness community that begins to influence and shape you into becoming an athlete. Maybe you won't keep gaining weight if you keep going for a walk. Once you see the pattern, you can defeat the weapon.

Now, go ahead, and give this a shot. Are you often angry, fighting with your spouse, and feeling like you want to give up? What might be causing that? Where was that behavior taught to you? What interpretations might your mind be running on autopilot that are causing you more pain? Map it out, and if you're feeling ambitious, break the chain with a new thoughtful response. If you're feeling brave and want to share your breakthrough with others who might be going through similar challenges, then post on social media what weapon you detected, what pattern you found, and how you broke your kill chain. Use the hashtag #weaponsofmassdeception, so I can celebrate with you.

MY KILL CHAIN

Fields of Formation:
_____
_____

Critical Experiences:
_____
_____

Passive Interpretations:
_____
_____

Automated Actions:
_____
_____

Reinforced Results:
_____
_____

CHAPTER 15

SEEING THE SHIFT

> *"Whatever it is that you're holding on to that doesn't serve you, that doesn't help you, and that doesn't progress your life . . . let it go."*
> —Trent Shelton[43]

Should our performance dictate our value? How do we connect with our best selves during our worst moments? What has been triggering our unwanted reactions? Too many leaders are destroying their lives from the inside out based on what they assume is "normal." They believe all high-level leaders feel an unending pressure to perform and an unresolved anxiety to prove to others how valuable they are, so that's what they allow in their life.

Even if that's the norm, is that what you want for your life? Do you want this to be your norm?

---

[43] Trent Shelton, "Protect Your Peace," 10 Aug. 2022, 21:05, *YouTube*, https://www.youtube.com/watch?v=g55OsM0v-E0.

There is no greater way to destroy the peace in your home than to harbor this pressure in your heart.

> THERE IS NO GREATER WAY TO DESTROY THE PEACE IN YOUR HOME THAN TO HARBOR THIS PRESSURE IN YOUR HEART.

Like most leaders, the pressure of performance is most likely a weapon that has been causing you to be unpleasant, easily irritated, and on edge. It's the reason you feel like you're going to snap while you run around, putting out fires at home and work and destroying your influence and ability to experience life the way you were meant to.

People don't want to be around someone who is always hurried and scattered. They won't follow someone who never has time for them and is always rushing to the next thing. When you map out the kill chain and analyze its pattern, you'll see how close you are to being free of this weapon. Identify common environments and situations that cause you to feel this way, and then, either change the environment or change your response. A little bit of intentionality and mindfulness can go a long way toward defeating this weapon.

PRESSURE OF PERFORMANCE KILL CHAIN

Let's take a look at a possible kill chain for the pressure of performance. As we do, think about what it could look like in your life. Does any of this relate to you? Does it inspire you to look into this yourself? Let that inspiration lead you. Follow that impulse.

Scenario: Good Enough

Michael's parents are stern and demanding. Despite the fact that Michael gets good grades and is on the first string of his high school's basketball team, they don't praise him. His achievement is pretty much just expected, and often, it's not enough. Michael receives an award at his school, and his parents don't even show up for the ceremony. Michael figures if he can just be good enough, eventually, they'll notice he's better than they think. He's constantly running. Never stopping. Trying to prove his value to his parents. Striving to hear that he is enough. Before he knows it, he is an unhealthy thirty-five-year-old father of three kids. He never smiles. He is always tense and easily irritated with the people around him. Everyone in his home feels the pressure. The weapon is robbing him and his family of desperately needed peace.

> **Fields of Formation**: Parents
> **Critical Experiences**: Constant criticism, overly high expectations, brief acknowledgment of success.
> **Passive Interpretations**: *I am only as valuable as my latest performance and measurements. If I do more, maybe I'll matter.*
> **Automated Actions**: Treadmill of performance.
> **Reinforced Results**: Exhaustion, chronic stress, grows into an unhealthy adult.

LESSONS LEARNED

Even though my critical experience did not mirror Michael's, I interpreted events in the same way. I no longer believe my performance determines my value. I don't try to prove to people that they should be proud of me. Once I analyzed the pattern, I could see areas where I would shift from peace to pressure and times when I would see a rise in stress or an upcoming deadline. This often involved trying to cram in a bunch of work or being stuck in a tunnel of focus when I was around my family. Because different things around me would try to break my focus or shift my attention, they would frustrate me and bring out unwanted reactions. After seeing this, I could design and deploy new ways of responding going forward. I began to put boundaries in place with my use of my phone and even my mind.

Time is your friend. As you dismantle the weapon, redesign your thought processes, and reconstruct your approach, allow yourself time to develop new habits. It took over a year for me to live free of this weapon, but as I broke the kill chain, I learned that time is my friend. Today, I feel good. I am still growing, still expanding, and not willing to be satisfied with anything less than God's best. But I also refuse to believe that I need to rush and hurry in order to prove to myself or anyone else that I am worthy or valuable.

What is your kill chain, and what pattern do you need to disrupt or agreement do you need to break? If you can see it, you can defeat it.

CHAPTER 16
PRIORITIZING OUR PEOPLE

"You will teach them to fly but they will not fly your flight. You will teach them to dream but they will not dream your dream. You will teach them to live but they will not live your life. Nevertheless in every flight, in every life, and every dream, the print of the way you taught them will always remain."
—Mother Teresa

Many streams of thought in the church teach that ambition is bad. I'm not really aligned with that. God created us to expand and lead our territories. We can still go out and change the world. We just need to open our eyes to the opportunities for life-changing impact and transformation right in front of us.

As a man of ambition who's spent time in prayer, I feel God has made it very clear that He is the One who gave me ambition, and it is for a purpose. But I've also learned that I need to be aware of times when my ambitious desires remove my availability for greater assignments. Ambition can bring destruction if it's manipulated by a weapon of mass deception. I speak from a place of love and understanding because it nearly wrecked my world.

After dismantling this weapon, I've learned to constantly live my life on mission while also expanding my perspective to see the people right in front me. I've learned to *Prioritize My People*: my family, friends, neighbors, coworkers, employees, and clients. Sometimes, this involves leaving my home for a weekend to speak at an event or putting some boundaries in place to enjoy protected time with my girls, and I've developed the following perspective: both places deserve the best version of myself.

I'm convinced, though, that my greatest place of *irreplaceable impact* is right within the four walls of my home. Someone else can lead my team at work. Someone else can show up and run a presentation on leadership. But no one else can show up and lead my family the way I can. No one. That's my assignment and my place of irreplaceable impact. This might sound intense, but we cannot afford to abdicate our ability to impact our children and spouse because we are viewing our responsibilities at home as obligations instead of assignments.

WE CANNOT AFFORD TO ABDICATE OUR ABILITY TO IMPACT OUR CHILDREN AND SPOUSE BECAUSE WE ARE VIEWING OUR RESPONSIBILITIES AT HOME AS OBLIGATIONS INSTEAD OF ASSIGNMENTS.

It's possible that what we view as an obligation, our family views with anticipation. In other words, driving your daughter to school might be out of the way for you and add time to your commute, but she might see this as the highlight of her day. She might anticipate that time with you. I'm learning this one the hard way, so just a tip from a fellow parent—give them your best.

Assignments come with an empowering grace from God. If God shared His children (your spouse and kids) with you to steward and serve, you are blessed.

My second child, Aspen Faith Jones, entered the world at the beginning of 2022. She's as beautiful and powerful as her big sister, Adalynne Grace Jones. Gotta throw the middle names in every once in a while, right? I'm blessed and honored to be a girl dad. I'm even more honored that God chose me to lead them. I get it if you're not a person of faith—no judgment at all. I just have to be real with you about who I am and what I believe. I believe this is one of the greatest assignments God could give me, but it's not about me. It's about them. In fact, the day we drove to the hospital for the scheduled delivery of Aspen, I remember sharing with my wife the following statement: "Jess, how cool is it that God is sending us Aspen? That she is being given to us by God for a specific reason? A friend of mine was praying about us and said he felt like God said a 'big bang' is coming. Could that be Aspen today?"

Now, here's the funny part. Guess what song she was born to. Out of the forty songs on our playlist, we added one last song to the group. She started to show up with the song "Gratitude" by Brandon Lake.[44] Then, for the final push and release into this world . . . we hear the

---

[44] Brandon Lake, vocalist, "Gratitude," by Benjamin Hastings, Brandon Lake, and Dante Bowe, released 3 Jun. 2022, track 7 on *House of Miracles*, Bethel Music—Tribl.

song "Bang!" by AJR begin to play. If you're not familiar, it goes: "Come hang. Let's go out with a bang. Bang! Bang! Bang!"[45]

We added the song to the labor playlist, but we could have never thought it would be the one to play perfectly for her birth. Yes, a big bang did arrive, just as my friend said. I'll never forget the laughter in the room as the delivery nurses, doctor, and Jess broke out into laughter as Aspen made her entrance. The most random song to play in a delivery room, and that's what my daughter was born to. Hilarious.

The levels of service and impact that you can make with your kids are like no others, and we can't make the same mistake Captain and then Chief Brown made, described in chapter 9. If you already have some drift, you can correct course. You might feel over your head and like being a parent can be a rat race. No one gave you a training manual. You might not have had the best examples. Unfortunately, this is the case for most of the high-performing leaders I meet. I'm shocked to see how many young people are searching for a father or a mother figure today.

As a leadership coach, I meet grown men and women who can't seem to figure out this whole "parenting" thing. Why? Well, kids have a mind of their own—literally—but I also believe most parents are looking for an example themselves. For me, there is no better example than my heavenly Father. He has never let me down.

We've talked about not having good examples. What about no example? The *lack* of parenting—whether it's due to divorce, neglect, abandonment, incarceration, illness, death, or estrangement—has a huge impact on the lives of children who grow into men and women left with a void in their hearts.

---

45 Jack Met, main vocals, "Bang!" by Adam Met, Jack Met, and Ryan Met, released 12 Feb. 2020, track 7 of *OK Orchestra*, AJR–BMG.

Impact.

It's right there in front of you.

It's hard.

It takes an act of courage to step up and play with a Barbie doll, Buzz Lightyear, or Lego set, knowing that the other work can be taken care of later. It takes a decision to show an act of love to your spouse and set aside consistent time to grow your relationship. It takes intentionality to remind your children who they are in the eyes of God.

Just last night, I was awakened four separate times—two of them were from our newborn, little Miss Aspen, who needed milk and a diaper change. The other two, surprisingly, were from our three-year-old, Adalynne. As I dragged myself out of bed and into Addy's room, I was shocked when I heard her request. Normally, if she wakes up in the middle of the night, it's because she is sick, needs a new braid for her hair, has dropped one of her 8,700 stuffed animals from her bed, or wants more milk. But this request was different. That night's request was, "Daddy. Sing, 'Come What May'?"

Wait, she woke me up at 2:00 a.m. to sing, "Come What May"?[46]

Alright, I'm about to lose any sense of "masculine" expectation that you might have had for me, but I've felt a deep connection to this song and my daughter from the time she was born. I'm not about the movie, but the song and this commitment that no matter what happens, "I will love you until my dying day" just felt so appropriate for our Addy Daddy Time. I sang it to her just about every day for three years. I know; I'm a big softy. That night, I thought to myself, *Wow. She gets it. She is connecting to this song. She knows her dad will love her forever—no matter what.* As I sang the words, I slowly tickled her face as she drifted back to sleep.

---

[46] Nicole Kidman and Ewan McGregor, vocalists, "Come What May," by David Baerwald, released 24 Sep, 2001, track 11 on *Moulin Rouge! Music from Baz Luhrmann's Film,* Interscope—Fox.

Can you see the irreplaceable impact? This is significant. This is something no one else can do. This is an assignment. God sent these girls to me and trusted me to be their father for a reason. He connected me to my amazing wife for reasons greater than I could ever imagine. How about you? Did you ever stop to thank God for His children and His trust in you as their earthly parent and steward? If not, do it now. I'll wait.

I can't believe how much energy I get as I write this chapter. It's strange how the thing I sucked at most has become the subject I find myself most excited to share. Just a few years ago, I was on a path that would have, one day, led to the destruction of my family. I said yes to everything, and I was unknowingly sacrificing my family on the altar of impact. This weapon of mass deception was destroying the fabric of my marriage and my family.

A huge shift happened for me when I began to see my wife differently too. I realized she is the greatest gift of all because she is exactly who I need in order to become who I was created to be. Her strengths are my weakness. My strengths complement her challenges. It's one thing to know that; it's another thing to see it. I can clearly see her for who she is, and I love it! I love how she brings balance to my life and how she helps me become more present each day we are together. I love that she loves to plan things because . . . I hate planning *so* much. I can see that in the pattern of my weapon, I was believing a lie. I thought my wife was slowing me down. The truth is that she was waking me up. She has awakened me to the life all around me.

I meet way too many good women and men who silence their voices and choose the path of least resistance in their marriage. Earn your spouse's love. I get that every relationship is different, but is it possible that you haven't even touched the surface of what is possible in your marriage? As we give love, we'll receive love. Give everything you have, dismantle your weapons, and watch what happens next.

Just another thought: what if you were assigned your spouse so that you could help them become who God created them to be?

WHAT IF YOU WERE ASSIGNED YOUR SPOUSE SO THAT YOU COULD HELP THEM BECOME WHO GOD CREATED THEM TO BE?

Success is seen by most as the accumulation of wealth, materials, people, or opportunities. But I love this definition of success from author Mark Batterson who has made such a huge impact in my life through his books. Mark says that his personal definition of success is like this: When those who know you best respect you most. Success starts with those who are closest to you. At the end of the day, I want to be famous in my home. And by the way, it's hard to be famous in your home if you're never home. If you succeed at the wrong thing, you've failed. If you fail at the right thing, you've succeeded.[47]

It's not good for us to be alone. Don't allow this weapon to bring you into isolation and cause you to drift from your family. It might destroy more than just your marriage.

ALTAR OF IMPACT KILL CHAIN

Scenario

Will was raised to believe there is no greater service than joining the military. He sees how everyone in his family who served is viewed with respect; therefore, he joins the military and completes his first,

---

[47] Mark Batterson, "The Homing Instinct," *YouTube,* 1 Jun. 2017, https://www.youtube.com/watch?v=DOIve5e3SN8&t=142s

second, and third deployment. He is soaring through the ranks but drifting from his family. One night, Will's wife asks him if he is packed for their marriage retreat. He had totally forgotten about it, planned another training, and can't cancel it. He realizes that while he forgot the marriage retreat, he honestly saw this as a waste of time. He thinks his unit can't handle life without him and that he needs to be there—even though he could use the leave he's accrued.

His wife attends the retreat without him. He continues to miss dates, half-listen to his wife and kids during dinnertime conversations, and is often unavailable for his family. He isn't trying to hurt them; he just wants to make sure his life counts and that he is there for the people who need him "most." He believes his most effective way of helping others is by leaving his family. He's going through the motions, and he can't seem to snap out of it. His wife eventually divorces him and moves across the country to live near her parents. The husband was never present and seemed to only give his family his leftovers.

> **Fields of Formation:** Family, military
> **Critical Experiences:** Family members who've served in the military get treated with the most respect.
> **Passive Interpretations:** *If I want to make a difference in the world and be worthy of respect, I must put my military career first.*
> **Automated Actions:** Continues to prioritize his military unit over his immediate family.
> **Reinforced Results:** He loses his family completely.

LESSONS LEARNED

Anything that is intended to harm us can actually teach us a valuable lesson. Often what is being attacked reveals what our greatest strength is. That's why it's being targeted.

I learned that these weapons were using my ambition to destroy my influence with my family as I continually sacrificed them on the altar of impact. It's possible the same could be happening to you. My ambition to make an impact in the world was blocking my ability to respond to greater assignments in my life. Only after dismantling this weapon could I see that my ambition had to be aligned with my assignment. I could stay ready for when God says, "Go!" and leave space in my schedule to say yes.

The slightest course correction can change your trajectory and eventually your destination. Make that correction now. Start by setting one new boundary that will protect your assignment. I asked a few high-performing leaders to share some pointers regarding their family leadership. They shared the following:

> "No meetings scheduled after 5:00 p.m. From 5 to 8, I'm with my family, and I'm a fully present [parent] to my kids."
> "Saturdays are off-limits. Family time only. I'm not a planner. I like to go with the flow. I learned if I just partner with my wife by telling her the days we should do something, she loves to plan and figure out the rest."
> "Each month, I take a day off during the week and date my husband. It's a game-changer. Neither one of us wants to miss out on those days."
> "I don't raise my hand for every new opportunity to lead a mission. I realized that over time, I'm not giving any of the younger leaders a chance to get their boots dirty."

When you detect the influence of the altar of impact, you must disrupt the pattern, break the kill chain, and look into the eyes of those closest to you. Notice how much they need you; it will give you all the courage you need to fight for them.

Just a heads up: your family might need to adjust to this new version of you. They truly could have some PTSD from the past and might take a few weeks or months to warm up to your new mindset, but it will come together. If you need help, reach out to someone you trust! It's going to be okay; it just takes time.

I no longer make my greatest level of impact by leaving home. Yes, this is one manifestation of my gift, and I love traveling to speak and train leaders to build transformational teams, but I also love family Friday. I love date day. I can't wait for our pizza nights. These aren't distractions pulling me from my purpose. They are elements of my purpose displayed in the simplest moments.

Analyze your kill chain. What tacit agreement do you need to break? If you can see it, you can destroy it.

CHAPTER 17

OWNING OUR STORY

"Be a light, not a judge. Be a model, not a critic. Be part of the solution, not part of the problem."
—Stephen R. Covey[48]

One thing can steal your joy.

One thing can cause you to doubt, overthink, and underappreciate every step of progress in your life.

One thing can cause you to see the accomplishments of others with envy instead of excitement.

The cycle of comparison.

Did you ever get asked about your time in the service and feel ashamed about what you never did? Have you ever been told, "Thank you for your service," but your mind begins to tell you that you didn't really do enough to receive that appreciation? You're not alone. This isn't just your mind; it's a weapon trying to steal your joy, and it runs rampant through our world.

---
[48] Stephen R. Covey, *7 Habits of Highly Effective People* (New York, NY: Simon & Schuster Ltd, 2020).

I find that this is often tied to expectations that you had that were never fulfilled. Which is why you feel it was never enough. Maybe you expected to join the service and become a battle-hardened combat veteran, but instead, you stayed within our border, and most of your time was spent behind a desk organizing administrative records. The expectation gap is one thing that is causing you to feel the pain caused by the cycle of comparison.

Social media has only magnified the cycle's ability to bring destruction. You probably see this weapon targeting your loved ones, but are you seeing how it's been attacking you? The lives of so many amazing men and women are limited because, according to the world—or even themselves—they haven't accomplished anything "significant."

The cycle of comparison causes you to compare your worst day to someone else's best day. Where did this weapon originate? How do we destroy the cycle of unceasing comparison to others? I think you will find it's easier than you think, but it will take more focus than ever before.

When we view the possible kill chain of the cycle of comparison listed below, you'll notice that it always connects to a sense of lack and insecurity being reinforced through someone else's achievement. I'm not sure if you know this, but you can't be a Navy SEAL and an Army officer in the same moment. You can't deploy for five years and stay home for five years during the same time period. You can't live someone else's story. It's your story to live, your chapters to write, and your decisions to make.

It might sound simple and obvious, but we can't live two lives.

Let's look at a simple but typical kill chain that many of our kids are experiencing and that often follows them into adulthood.

CYCLE OF COMPARISON KILL CHAIN

Scenario

Katie is a teenager. She has waited what seems like forever to be allowed by her parents to open social media accounts: Facebook, Twitter, Instagram, etc. She knows she has friends, and it's high time she got some recognition. She starts posting pictures of herself and her pets. She's gotten quite a few likes. However, Sierra just posted pictures of herself in a new outfit and is experiencing rapid growth and likes. Yes, the outfit is a bit revealing, but it's the style. Katie decides to do the same thing. She posts more videos that show her in similar revealing outfits. Her views and followers are increasing, and it feels great. But with each action, she feels less appreciated for who she really is, losing herself in the likes and follows. Over time, she begins to believe she is only accepted when she pretends to be someone else.

> **Fields of Formation**: Friends, society
> **Critical Experiences**: Sierra's posts of her revealing outfit garners more "likes" than Katie's posts, so Katie posts similar pictures.
> **Passive Interpretations**: *People will only "like" me when I dress like Sierra.*
> **Automated Actions**: Katie's posts get more revealing to get more "likes."
> **Reinforced Results**: Katie loses the value she used to feel just by being herself.

If all we see is what we don't have or what we haven't done—but other people do have or have done—then we'll never have enough or do enough to experience any level of fulfillment. We can't defeat the cycle of comparison by just *getting more* or *doing more* because when we reach the next level, we'll only see what we still don't have. This is why we can find someone with an audience of a million followers on social media feeling depressed and discouraged. It just wasn't enough to fill them. To start defeating this weapon, we've got to accept responsibility for our story and then accept that the story isn't over yet.

TO START DEFEATING THE CYCLE OF COMPARISON, WE'VE GOT TO ACCEPT RESPONSIBILITY FOR OUR STORY AND THEN ACCEPT THAT THE STORY ISN'T OVER YET.

Is it possible that what you have is enough? Is it possible that even though you don't lead a large organization, you are still reaching millions of people through your one life? How many apple trees are in one apple seed anyway? We never know, do we?

You weren't designed to be anyone other than who you are. You are not your thoughts. You are not the weapon. You have been uniquely designed for a reason, and it's often far greater than what you can see today. Your story is YOUR story, and I think one of the best things you can do is just own it. When you own your story, you embrace the lessons and the rewards that are hidden within it.

Let's say you were kicked out of the military or college or a professional association. One of your actions didn't comply with the standards. That sucks, but it is just one part of your story. The story isn't over yet, so what can you learn from this experience?

Recently, I was invited to participate in a business leadership mastermind in Pittsburgh called Auxano. This event was phenomenal. As the lead facilitator Kyle Stark mentioned, the room was filled with blackbelt players with white belt mentalities. It was the perfect combination of hungry but humble leaders who were looking to level up and add value to others. I rubbed shoulders with some outstanding professional athletes, coaches, business leaders, and entrepreneurs. During one of our group brainstorming sessions, the USA men's volleyball coach shared four words that a high-performance trainer taught his team. I don't think I'll ever forget them.

So what? Now what?

We lost the game. So what? Now what?

This phrase reminds me of two words we learned in the service: *Continue Mission*. So you didn't get the position you wanted? Continue Mission. So you failed the last test? Continue Mission. So you just got promoted? Congratulations! Continue Mission.

You lost your license through a DUI? So what? Now what?

Your marriage is falling apart, and you can't keep a job? So what? Now what?

You aren't big enough to play in the NFL? So what? Now what?

You never served in the military. So what? Now what?

How are you going to respond to adversity? Will you hang your head low, or will you grit your teeth and continue mission?

The cycle of comparison has been whispering, "You're not really a veteran, a leader, a winner, an innovator, a coach. You're not really a good man or a good woman. If only they knew the real you, they would hate you." And here's the worst part about it. This weapon doesn't speak from a second-person perspective. Instead, it sounds just like you. It's so tightly woven and hidden in your thoughts that it has disguised itself to sound just . . . like . . . you.

Which is how it causes you to think:

I'm not really a veteran.

I'm not really a leader.

I'm not really an inspiration to other people.

I'm not really a role model or a good parent.
If they only knew who I really am, they wouldn't accept me.

Would you talk to someone else the way you talk to yourself? Probably not. You probably wouldn't even let another person talk to you that way. This begs the question, are you really the voice talking trash to yourself, or is it the weapon? I vote for the latter.

Inspirational speaker and author of *The Infinite Game* Simon Sinek stated in a recent interview:

Look. Human beings—we can't help but compare ourselves to others. Comparison is the deadliest thing we can do to ourselves because we will always come up short. All it does is exaggerate all of our insecurities. It's okay to enjoy other people's success, but let them live their lives, and you live your life.[49]

To add to this idea, I would share that I believe there are times when healthy comparison can actually help you. When we compare achievements, appearances, and audiences, we will always feel discouraged and inadequate. But when we compare things such as attitude or mindset, we should feel challenged to grow. I don't know about you, but I actually want to see someone who demonstrates a strong and resilient attitude. I want to compare to see if I haven't been as positive as I could be at this time of my life. I want to be inspired by people who are mentally tough. I love reminding myself that I can improve in areas, but if you notice something, these are mainly choices connected to a progression—not achievements connected to significance.

---

[49] Simon Sinek, "The Most Destructive Self Habit," *YouTube* interview, 20 Mar. 2021, https://www.youtube.com/watch?v=jtpOYxsZj7o.

WE DO NOT ALL HAVE THE SAME PURPOSE FOR OUR LIFE, BUT EVERY LIFE IS SIGNIFICANT.

We do not all have the same purpose for our life, but every life is significant.

I'm sure it's fine to compare your progress to other people's progress if it will help you grow and feel inspired. However, I bet this causes you to feel deflated, right? Right. So, that's not helping anyone.

Life strategist Ed Mylett shares a powerful perspective regarding the danger of this weapon. He explains that he learned not to compare who he is today with any previous form of who he was before because he recognizes that stages of life change. If you think about it, comparing your marriage of five years to how it felt during the first five months isn't a fair comparison. Mylett continues to say, "Comparison is a formula for misery."[50]

Don't miss this. It might sound like an oversimplification, but I think what most of us really want is just to be happy and to know our life matters. This weapon tells us that we aren't happy, but it promises us happiness by getting us to believe, *When I have what they have, then I can feel what they feel.*

This could sound like the following:

> When I have more money than he does, I will feel happy like he does.
> When my business is as big as hers, then I can feel just as confident.

---

[50] Ed Mylett, "Comparison Is a Formula for Misery! | Ed Mylett Motivation," *YouTube* shorts, 18 Feb. 2022, https://www.youtube.com/shorts/lI4CQY2eROA.

> If I have a sports car, I can be happy.
> If I had the starting position on the team, I could be happy.
> If I were an Army Ranger, then I would be skilled, brave, strong... enough.

What the weapon is hiding is that happiness and these other core feelings come *before* the achievement. Just read Holocaust survivor Victor Frankl's famous book, *Man's Search for Meaning*. Frankl states:

Don't aim at success. The more you aim at it and make it a target, the more you are going to miss it. For success, like happiness, cannot be pursued; it must ensue, and it only does so as the unintended side effect of one's personal dedication to a cause greater than oneself or as the by-product of one's surrender to a person other than oneself. Happiness must happen, and the same holds for success: you have to let it happen by not caring about it.[51]

Is it possible that happiness and fullness actually attract achievement? If so, then the cycle of comparison—which causes us to delay happiness—thwarts our achievement. It prevents us from reaching those dreams.

As a man of faith, I remember learning that we who follow Christ are called to constantly expand our influence—not so people will believe what we believe, but so they will experience the peace, joy, and love that comes with our leadership. Most Christians that I saw growing up were fearful and judgmental. Something about that didn't make sense. In Genesis 1, the first chapter of the Bible, it says that God created man to have dominion over the fish of the sea, the birds of the air, the cattle, the earth, and every creeping thing that creeps on the earth. It also says that we were given instruction to be fruitful, multiply, fill the earth and subdue it.

---

[51] Viktor E. Frankl, et al, *Man's Search for Meaning* (Boston, MA: Beacon Press, 2006).

In the New Testament, it states that God is love. This means that the core essence of God is love. So my belief shifted after dismantling this weapon, and I began to see how we were meant to be led by love. Moved by compassion, not comparison. We were built to *expand,* but this weapon will cause us to shift our focus from expansion to envy. It will cause us to feel discouraged by the success of others instead of inspired. But what if instead of *comparing,* we *collaborated*? What if we were driven to partner with each other, fully recognizing that we cannot be all things to all people. What if we could see others expand and be inspired by that growth instead of discouraged?

WE WERE BUILT TO EXPAND, BUT THE CYCLE OF COMPARISON WILL CAUSE US TO SHIFT OUR FOCUS FROM EXPANSION TO ENVY.

Is it as simple as controlling our focus?

Just because we are growing—we're not there yet . . . we haven't "arrived"—it doesn't mean we should be grumpy and bitter. Honestly, you might not have the position or influence that you want to have yet. But that doesn't mean you have to be an angry leader. You can still grow, you can still expand, and you can still be inspired by others, but when you place your focus on someone else for too long, you begin to idolize their life. Therefore, you lose your joy,

Life is a pilgrimage of progress. Let's find a way to celebrate that progress both for ourselves and those around us. Agreed? See, this weapon would hate for you to believe what I just said because the truth about humanity is that we are better together. We are brighter together. We are bigger together.

I remember being told about great military officers and their programs that I should check out, considering my business. Quickly, I would shift from being inspired to feeling inadequate. The more videos I watched, the more I felt that my voice, story, and message didn't matter anymore. I felt that since I didn't have the same qualifications, I couldn't add any more value to the topic. What I didn't realize was that we live in a world of abundance. The same lessons taught by a different voice in a different manner can connect with a different person.

We all make a unique sound in this world, so our job is to release that sound—not to be an echo. Much of our world is filled with echoes instead of unique sounds because the cycle of comparison has been dissuading and delaying others. People say the same thing, the same way, just for more views and more followers. People who just repeat what others have said in order to play it safe. There is tremendous value in modeling habits and lessons after others, but when it comes time to create—to write your own story—copying will not get the job done.

THE SAME LESSONS TAUGHT BY A DIFFERENT VOICE CAN CONNECT WITH A DIFFERENT PERSON.

Maybe the whole time you've been reading, you've been thinking that your story doesn't sound anything like mine. Or maybe it sounds so much like mine that it's not really yours. Here's what I think about that: Shut that down right now! Your story is your story. Only you can live it, and only you can tell it. At this point, you were not meant to . . . *whatever*. So what? Now what? Continue Mission. Right?

Your story can still be greater than you can imagine. But you've got to dismantle the cycle of comparison. This weapon hates you and wants you to live paralyzed by your past. The decisions you have made are decisions you must accept. But today, right now, in this moment, with your next decision, you can change your destiny. And by the way, *somebody's destiny is tied to your next decision*. Who might that be?

LESSONS LEARNED

As a representative of the infamous "Joneses," let me speak to the common phrase "Keeping up with the Joneses." The significance of this phrase is tied to the relative position of another person. The Joneses are the neighbors. You see them every day. Their yard looks perfect. Their family is always dressed in a coordinated effort. They're never late. And they are just close enough to you to compare yourself with them but far enough away for you to always feel behind. But let me ask you: Do you even want what they have? Do you really want the latest luxury car, Coach bag, or perfectly landscaped lawn? Does your spouse really want that, or was it something they were taught?

I recently stumbled on a talk by Luke Burgis, the author of *Wanting*. Luke explains a concept called mimetic desire. He says:

By definition, mimetic desire means that we're adopting another person's desire as our own, usually without even realizing that we're doing it. Social media has given us millions of mimetic models that we now have to contend with. Some people have gone from having 10 mimetic models to now having thousands, and we haven't quite come to grips as a culture with what that means for our mental and emotional health. All desire comes from us feeling like we lack something, which can bring us into a dangerous, vicious habit because there will always be another model to find. We have to choose our models wisely whether they are famous influencers across the globe or our closest friends. We also have to know when the model is inflaming us with the desire for something that's going to bring real fulfillment or whether it's going to bring a dopamine hit or allow us to fantasize about a life that we'll probably never have. All desires are modeled for us 24 hours a day, billions of them, and we need to understand the mimetic landscape of social media, or else we'll become completely controlled by it.[52]

Wow. Okay. Reading that last part made me quickly move from appreciating Luke's writing style to envying it. I'm serious. I was thinking, *Man, I wish I could sound as smart as he does when I'm explaining weapons of mass deception. Maybe this isn't going to be good enough.*

Isn't that crazy? The guy who is writing about the weapon is just as susceptible to its influence as you. That's why we must train ourselves to detect the very onset of its temptations because it constantly appears at the slightest hint of feelings of inadequacy. Now, how did I stop the weapon from firing? Well, as a man of faith, I know who I am in Christ, I know what I bring to the table, I know who I'm meant to help, and I'm sure that Luke is just as great as I am.

When Coach Dabo Swinney took over as the interim head coach for Clemson football, he told his team, "We aren't going to worry about being the best. We are going to focus on being OUR best."[53] And then he showed them examples of what OUR best would look like. That's what I want you to remember: just be YOUR best. Easier said than done, I know, but you can train your mind.

---

[52] Luke Burgis, *Wanting: The Power of Mimetic Desire, and How to Want What You Need* (London: Swift Press, 2021).
[53] "How Dabo Swinney Changed the Culture of Football and Made Clemson a Winner," interview with Ed Mylett, *YouTube*, 15 June 2021, https://www.youtube.com/watch?v=sey5_87-XWY.

Study your triggers. Begin studying when you shift from comparing what you don't have to comparing what you do have. *You might want to read that again.* We don't destroy the cycle of comparison by comparing *again.* Do you see what I'm saying? Most people see someone who is crazy jacked. They look down at their belly, they think about how much they suck, and then, they shift the comparison to a new feature. They say, "Yeah, he might be jacked. But he's probably a jerk." In other words, they make themselves feel better about what they perceive to be their inadequacy by imagining or pointing out someone else's inadequacy. This is why we call this weapon a CYCLE of comparison. It doesn't stop unless we stop. In the example, that guy didn't destroy the cycle of comparison. He deferred it, giving it more time to grow. All he did was shift the comparison of one feature where he fell short to an area where he could be the obvious winner.

As a leadership consultant, one thing I teach organizations during my workshops is that we don't build the tallest tower by tearing everyone else's down. That's how we build enemies. Rick Warren, in his book *The Purpose Driven Life*, talked about how C.S. Lewis said, "True humility is not thinking less of yourself, it's thinking of yourself less."[54]

Hopefully, you've begun to see the fragility of this weapon. It often ties to your focus and your motives. I've found that if we slow down to appreciate our unique story and allow ourselves to see the distinctive value in each person around us, the weapon begins to collapse. Gratitude and appreciation shatter the effects of this weapon. When mapping out a kill chain, it's common to see a link in the chain that you can break—reverse its effects—with some intentionality and discipline.

---

[54] Rick Warren, *The Purpose Driven Life: What on Earth Am I Here for?* (Grand Rapids, MI: Zondervan, 2021).

You can find an unspoken agreement that you've made with a deceptive idea, and you can break this agreement to weaken the weapon.

Often our kill chain is tied to those passive interpretations that we have allowed to guide us to experience a reality that we wouldn't desire. In the final part of this book, you'll receive some practical tactics that you can deploy right away to combat this weapon, but for now allow this moment and this chapter to expose the pattern of this weapon as you learn to operate in a greater state of peace, power, and purpose today. If you can see it, you can defeat it.

CHAPTER 18
BREAKING THE CEILING

"Remember that it is the actions, and not the commission, that make the officer, and that there is more expected from him, than the title."
—George Washington[55]

Who are you without the structure of the service, the corporation, the foundation, the rank, and the title you've relied on in the past? While you are still a high-performance leader, you are not necessarily an officer, an executive, a soldier, a cop, a firefighter, a pastor, a business owner, a medic, or a service member, depending on your background. These might be past positions that you can connect to for the next chapter of your story, but they are not your identity. Prior labels can be indicators of your purpose, but they must not be perceived as limits. See these experiences as foundations for you to build on top of—not ceilings for you to be limited by.

---

[55] "Address to the Officers of the Virginia Regiment - Thursday, January 08, 1756," *George Washington's Mount Vernon*, https://www.mountvernon.org/library/digitalhistory/quotes/article/remember-that-it-is-the-actions-and-not-the-commission-that-make-the-officer-and-that-there-is-more-expected-from-him-than-the-title/.

I'm going to keep this chapter short since this is already a well-known weapon, and your awareness alone will begin to weaken the weapon and its kill chain. If you want to dive deeper into this topic, feel check out my site where I have a few podcast episodes linked: adamfjones.com/podcast.

Unfortunately, the trap of title has influenced way too many people and only seems to evolve as time continues. Let's break it down and see what could be causing this.

TRAP OF TITLE KILL CHAIN

Scenario 1: What a Waste!

Wayne is raised with significant respect for rank and titles. As a child, he is drawn to military movies. He sees how they highlight leaders in high-level positions and even civilians in a company or organization. Today, he is a highly respected colonel in the Marines. After twenty years of service, he retires and begins life as a civilian. Immediately, he notices that people don't recognize his experience in the same way. When he describes the work he did in the Marines, people can't relate. He can't believe how out of place he feels. It's like they don't see the value he could add and what he is capable of. He feels tolerated instead of celebrated. Instead of developing his influence as a civilian, he rests on his past success and compartmentalizes his life. He lives as a Marine without a uniform and can't connect with others. Without the structure of the service and the norms of the service, he no longer knows how to operate. He loses his confidence and sense of power. He argues with his family and those he works with. And he has started drinking to get through it.

> **Fields of Formation**: Family, movies, television, the military
> **Critical Experiences**: Retires from his career in the military.

> **Passive Interpretations**: *I'm no one. This is pointless. I have no purpose.*
> **Automated Actions**: Compartmentalizes his life and rests on past successes.
> **Reinforced Results**: Loses confidence and feels increasingly alienated from those at home and work.

Scenario 2: All in the Family

Elizabeth is a go-getter. She is the youngest of five children, and her parents had her later in life, so her brothers and sisters have graduated high school and then college, gotten married, had children, and are well-established in their careers. It seemed easy for them, and she follows in their footsteps. She is a successful, well-respected professional in her field, wife, mother of two, and the primary breadwinner in her home. Her friends call her Wonder Woman.

Then, two months ago, Elizabeth almost passed out when giving a presentation. Her heart and head pounded, she felt dizzy, and she sat down and closed her eyes before taking a few deep breaths. When she stood up, she realized she had lost sight in her right eye. Doctors said physically she was fine. Her symptoms were a manifestation of the mental stress she was under. Her career and life—as she knew them—were over. None of her siblings had experienced this. What was wrong with her? Instead of letting her family rally around her and help, she buckles down and insists she can push through. Her doctors fear she's headed for a stroke. Wonder Woman, indeed!

> **Fields of Formation**: Family, friends
> **Critical Experience**: Physical manifestation of mental stress resulting in excruciating headaches and loss of complete sight.

- > **Passive Interpretation**: *I need to follow the path of the others in my family.*
- > **Automated Actions**: Compares her accomplishments and experience with her siblings' and finds herself lacking.
- > **Reinforced Results**: Pushes through at the expense of her health.

LESSONS LEARNED

The greatest lesson I learned from this weapon is that a title doesn't make a person. A person makes the title. If our title is what gives us a feeling of significance, then we lose the feeling when we lose the title. When you detect the trap of title, it's time to destroy how you relate to it. Realize that leadership is influence, not a title. Your title was important, but it is something to be leveraged—not limited by.

After I was discharged from the Army, I had to find new ways to appreciate the opportunity to reinvent myself and embrace a new challenge. I love that I used to be an Army captain. It's a great way to help others through the stories I've shared and experiences that I encountered. But this rank doesn't define who I am.

I am much more than a captain. I don't present myself to everyone as a pilot or as an Army guy. Instead, I just enjoy the conversation. I realized it's not an "Us vs. Them" mentality but a lack of understanding that causes a disconnect in relatability with civilians after the service. The people in your life most likely love hearing about your background, but they don't know how to relate. You have a choice. You can either make them feel uncomfortable and out of place, or you can allow yourself to grow and learn to connect in new ways without the title or uniform. If you see it, you can defeat it.

CHAPTER 19
MY NEW DECLARATION

I think it's time . . .

Time to decide . . .

Time to declare . . .

Would you join me as you decide and declare right now that you will break the agreement with each of these deceptions? There is nothing else you are waiting for. You just need to make a decision and then make it the right decision.

Release the truth. Speak. If God spoke, and He created the world, and if God spoke, and He created you, then I believe that when we speak, mountains move. It is time to speak. I'm going to get pretty spiritual on you here. If that offends you, feel free to skim through the next chapter because I can only speak about what I've done—not what I think I should do.

I broke my agreement with each weapon, and by doing so, I've achieved a level of freedom that I could have never imagined possible.

THE DECLARATION OF COMPLETE DEPENDENCE

Feel free to disagree, but I'm going to share the greatest secret I've ever learned to becoming entirely freed from all four weapons of mass deception. You might not like this, but I encourage you to give it a shot. I'm not forcing this on you, but I am going to share it. I hope that at this stage of our journey, you have learned that my heart is merely to help you and your family experience ultimate transformation.

Ready? Well, strap up; it's time to bring the domination of these weapons to an end.

A few years ago, I was attending a worship service with a select group of ministry and business leaders. Toward the end of the weekend, a question was asked to all of us but then, directly to me: "Will you give God your yes?"

I was already a follower of Christ, so he wasn't asking if I would accept Him into my life. Rather, he was asking if I would accept Him to lead my life. I remember unintentionally saying out loud, "But what if we don't know what we are saying yes to?"

My heart was racing. I wanted to say yes. I wanted to just give up control and allow Him to lead, but what if it hurt my marriage more? What if God was going to send me to some foreign country on a yearlong expedition that only made things worse for my family?

The ministry leader walked right up to me and calmly said, "We don't know what we are saying yes to." He paused and look at me in the eyes. "But we know He is a good, good Father, isn't He?"

Right away, I became aware of a great weight in my life. A weight that was holding me back from my next promotion. The stem of multiple weapons of mass deception. Control. I thought I needed to control everything.

I was afraid to trust friends, family, and God.

I wanted everything to fit in my box and my self-imposed structure. But none of this was giving me the life I wanted.

So I made a decision. I surrendered.

I surrendered to the leadership of Christ. I decided I would listen more carefully for His words in my heart. I knew if I had plans of accomplishment, He had a purpose for me to keep me available so that I would listen to Him.

Even as a Christian, I knew there was another level, and I wanted to go there with Him. I wanted my life to change lives. Until that point, I was really just practicing a religion. So I said yes. I let Him "take the controls," trusting that His destination is better than anything I could ever plan. Knowing that He joined my wife and me for a purpose. Knowing that He gave me our daughter (Aspen wasn't born yet) for a purpose.

And I trusted that He would preserve that purpose.

I had to surrender to the goodness of God.

I had to trust that His plans for my life were even greater than my ambitions.

This is the secret.

The goodness of God is what leads us to turn from our broken beliefs and mindsets—not some fear-based religious mantra, but a message of love, restoration, and goodness. Haven't you noticed that every kill chain starts with what someone else has taught you? I don't know about you, but I needed a new teacher. I needed to remove the pressure from my parents, my wife, my mentors, my friends, my family, and everyone else to be perfect models that I could learn from, and I had to choose THE PERFECT MODEL. It wasn't fair to everyone around me that I expected their perfection. It wasn't fair to them that I thought they needed to be someone they weren't in order to fill me.

In order for me to receive God as my leader, I had to release everyone else from my unreasonable expectations.

IN ORDER FOR ME TO RECEIVE GOD AS MY LEADER, I HAD TO RELEASE EVERYONE ELSE FROM MY UNREASONABLE EXPECTATIONS.

I couldn't reflect the image of a good, kind, loving father if I didn't receive the image of a good, kind, loving heavenly Father. I had to look at the life of Jesus.

The true and foolproof way to become a better man or woman is to learn from a better Man.

If you're hurting, I'm sorry.

If you had a rough start, it doesn't mean you have to have a failed ending.

If you have already lost some relationships, I'm right there with you, but life isn't over yet.

The love of God repairs and redeems all destruction from these weapons.

Nothing is lost.

You might have read these last chapters and thought it was too late for you. That you have already lost your marriage. You're already divorced multiple times. Your kids don't want anything to do with you. Your friends are gone. Your life is going nowhere. But I'm telling you; it's not over yet.

There is a mission for your life, and you must continue it. Only you can accomplish it because it's unique to you. It's your story, your influence, your relationships, your experience, and your location.

You must Continue Mission.

Your best days can be your next days, but you won't know that if you don't make a change.

As I type this out, I can feel the weight of your guilt and shame that have been hidden in the weapons.

I want you to know that it's all relative.

From the bottom of a *pit*, often, all we can often see is darkness.

But if we surrender to God, we will find the light.

If we follow our Lord, one day, we'll reach the top of a *peak*.

You are not too late.

The mission to bring transformation to your heart, home, and headquarters is still fully alive and stronger than ever.

Chaotic times reveal transformational leaders. This is when you are needed more than ever.

You can use this book as a tool to fight back. A tool to equip others. In fact, I encourage you to do exactly that. Get them their own copy, and let them know why you thought of them. Together, we can bring transformation just through an invitation.

When the weight of the world is on your shoulders, and you feel that all you see is darkness, open this up, and find the light.

If you are a high-performance man or woman, then you know what it's like to be led by a leader whom you respect and admire. I'm asking you to do that again.

Release what you are holding, receive a new Leader, and reveal a new life.

If you're ready to make a declaration of complete dependence, then join me in this next section.

MY DECLARATION OF COMPLETE DEPENDENCE

Lord, I am fully Yours.

I trust in Your goodness.

I trust in Your kindness.

I want Your good plans for my life, my spouse's life, and my kids' lives to be fulfilled through Your leadership in me.

I want to receive a new image.

I want to receive a new mission.

Commission me, Lord, with Your alignment and authority for something greater than I could ever have imagined.

Lord, I do not have all the answers, but I know that I choose You.

I know that I am one with the One who knows all things.

Lord, awaken in me who I truly was created to be.

Destroy the authority of the four weapons, and deploy the power of your solutions.

Today, I announce my complete dependence on You.

You are all that I need.

In Jesus's victorious name. Amen.

Whew.

Did you feel that, or was it just me?

I'm so proud of you, my friend.

Welcome to the family—the family of God.

You don't need to perform for this family. You don't need to hide from this family. You don't need to compete for this family. You only need to enjoy this family.

Now, if you just prayed that, this is just the start. I have a slight background in ministry—not sure if you figured that out yet—and I want you to know something that I tell anyone that I speak with regarding this subject: Salvation is just the start. Now, the fun begins. Welcome to the kingdom. In the kingdom, you have a unique role, authority, and opportunity to partner with God each day of your life to bring peace, joy, and love with you everywhere you go.

If you were already a follower of Christ, and you just gave Him leadership over your life, congratulations! It's about to get fun.

Honestly, it might sound weird, but when you focus on a relationship with God and allow Him to lead you, life becomes more fun than anything you've ever done. I call it *Spirit-Led Leadership*. There is nothing better.

Now, if you read all of this and just can't seem to accept that God is good, and He is for you, it's all good! I am here for you just the same. I just really needed to share with you the secret that unlocked all freedom for me. I'm not willing to be "fake" to make others comfortable. This was me just being real with you, and I want to thank you for not shutting me down because of my faith. I'm not some professional preacher or anything like that; it's just my story. So if that's you, and you want to learn more, I created some free resources. Go to adamfjones.com/faith. I've also developed some special trainings just for you. Again, I'm here for you regardless, but I sure would love for you to really experience this level of joy and transformation.

In fact, the book isn't even over yet!

So join me in our final phase where I will have the honor and privilege to equip you with some world-changing counterattacks!

PHASE 3 SUMMARY

KEY TERMS

- Trust Your Instruments
- Kill Chain—a predictable pattern of attack that weapons follow to bring destruction.
- Break the Kill Chain—breaking one link in a weapon's kill chain to defeat an attack sequence.
- Here is the Kill Chain for nearly every Weapon of Mass Deception:
    1) FIELDS OF FORMATION shape a person's language, perception, and mindset.
    2) CRITICAL EXPERIENCES conflict, confirm, or challenge a belief taught during formation.
    3) PASSIVE INTERPRETATIONS occur without someone noticing that their mind has rapidly sorted and assigned meaning to an experience.
    4) AUTOMATED ACTIONS subconsciously begin to guide behavior as the person repeatedly and unknowingly allows a hidden deception to lead them.
    5) REINFORCED RESULTS change a person's environment and beliefs, bringing widespread damage over a period of time.
- Declaration of Complete Dependence—no more trying to do this thing on your own.
- Progress Display Panel—practical method to measure trends and progress in your life.

KEY CONSIDERATIONS
- Four Keys to Correction
  1) Trust—Your feelings might be wrong. We must trust our instruments and the experiences of leaders around us.
  2) Order—Training is critical, and order matters. We must correct the issue in the right order.
  3) Connected—Everything is connected. For every action, there is a reaction.
  4) Intentional—Each corrective action should be smooth, coordinated, and deliberate.
- 4-I Instrument Framework
  1) Importance: Why does this instrument gauge matter to me?
  2) Indicators: What signals will show my current status and path?
  3) Instruction: What corrections should I make?
  4) Insight: What deeper understanding and lesson can come from this?
- Recommended Progress Display Panel
  1) Peace
  2) People
  3) Purpose
  4) Power

SUMMARY
When you see it, you can destroy it. When you see it, you can defeat it. The greatest strength of a weapon of mass deception is its secrecy. When you map out the kill chain for various challenges you continue to experience, you will see the weak link. It is here you will strike a blow to break the kill chain.

PHASE 4

DEPLOY THE COUNTERATTACK

*"The idea that a war can be won by standing on the defensive and waiting for the enemy to attack is a dangerous fallacy, which owes its inception to the desire to evade the price of **victory**."*
—Field Marshal Sir Douglas Haig, Commander of the British Army (1914-1918) (emphasis added) [56]

Fight and you may die. Run and you will live . . . at least awhile. And dying in your beds many years from now, would you be willin' to trade all the days, from this day to that, for one chance, just one chance, to come back here as young men and tell our enemies that they may take our lives but they will never take . . . OUR FREEDOM!
—William Wallace, aka Official Badass of Scotland[57]

---

56 The New York Times Co., *The European War* (New York, NY: The New York Times, 1919), 545.
57 Biography.com Editors, "11 Famous 'Braveheart' Quotes," *Biography.com*, 29 Sept. 2020, https://www.biography.com/news/braveheart-quotes-anniversary.

CHAPTER 20

DEPLOY THE TACTICS

Now that we've defined the weapon, detected the deception, and dismantled the weapon by disrupting the pattern, we can follow it up by deploying an aggressive and decisive counterattack to redesign your life.

We are going to pull these tactics from a strategy that I've developed called the Blue Sky Leadership Strategy. This strategy that I teach to high-performance organizations is perfectly designed to help you regain your influence one step at a time.

The most important aspect of deploying the counterattack is understanding the compound effect. Professional author and coach Darren Hardy says in his popular book *The Compound Effect*, "The Compound Effect is the principle of reaping huge rewards from a series of small, smart choices."[58]

In this chapter, I'll share with you the practical tactics—the series of small, smart choices that I used—to wage a counterattack against

---

58 Darren Hardy, *The Compound Effect* (Philadelphia, PA: Vanguard Press, 2010), 9.

each weapon. Our goal is not just to stop getting hit but to *hit back* with force and precision.

That said, here are some tactics I deployed against each weapon: Pressure of Performance, Altar of Impact, Cycle of Comparison, and Trap of Title. I hope they serve to inspire you to craft your own response as your journey continues.

PRESSURE OF PERFORMANCE COUNTERATTACK
Tactic #1: Silence

I know for a high-performance leader, running at the speed of sound, this sounds impossible, but it's critical. We need to schedule consistent time for quiet. As much as possible, I began to structure my life to start my day with ten minutes of silence. No reading, no working out, no journaling . . . just sipping coffee and sitting in silence. Ten minutes of a still mind and quiet thoughts.

This could sound troubling because you don't want to live in your own thoughts. That's exactly my point. Don't just entertain any thought that comes into your mind; not all thoughts are productive. Instead, consider shutting those thoughts down and just sitting in silence.

Attempt to sense the closeness of God in the stillness of the morning. This tactic is what enabled me to withstand the worst days of my life. When everything else felt like it was falling apart, eventually, I found peace in the silence. I also access this when stress attacks.

Recommended Action: How can you start with silence? How do you think it would help everyone around you? Start your day with ten minutes of silence, and watch what happens.

Tactic #2: Seek to Understand

I find that for many of us fighting against the pressure of performance, there is a common factor. People. People have pushed us into performance. At some point in our life, we began to try to prove to a PERSON that we are worthy. Now today, that weapon could be constantly reminding you of all that you aren't based on what a PERSON might have never said.

So here's what I think. There might be some people in your life that you need to understand, accept, and appreciate. In other words, I have found by working with hundreds of high-performing men and women that MANY of them felt a void from their dad—or lack of a dad. The way they were raised caused them to feel like they never measured up, so they constantly tried to prove "him" wrong and be the opposite of their dad. You know what this was doing?

It was crushing them.

So instead of living like this and just ignoring these people in your life, what if you approached this from a different angle? Who do you need to better understand, accept, or appreciate in your life?

Maybe your dad wasn't intentional with what he said or how he used his time with you. What if you began to understand that his behavior was not because of you, but that's just who he is? I bet if you asked other people in your life the same question about your father, they would say the same thing. Over time, I think you would understand that what you want your father to be isn't who he is. It's not because he doesn't love or appreciate you. It's probably because he has his own things he is fighting, and they are diminishing his ability to connect with you in the way you needed.

Is it possible that you could accept him for who he is, realizing that it would almost be selfish for you to expect him to be someone he isn't? And if that's the case, could we take it a step further and learn to appreciate that aspect of who he is and how it's actually helped you become who you are?

Recommended Action: Who do you need to understand, accept, and maybe even appreciate? What's the first step you can take to start that process? Is there someone you can talk to today to maybe get a different perspective of that person? Don't wait. Take action now.

Tactic #3: Strategic Awareness

Recognizing that a particular measurement was only a snapshot of what I did in the past leading up to that point was extremely freeing for me.

Okay, so I failed the two-mile run. That doesn't mean I'm a failure. It means I failed. This event is simply a reflection of the wings, pizza, and long nights in the office that I allowed to stop me from training. This measurement is just a reflection of how I lived the past few months, but it doesn't define me. On the other side of the coin, it's possible that I received a performance evaluation that said I'm the top leader in a unit. Again, this is based on my past performance. What am I doing today to continue growing?

When you receive a test score or performance evaluation at work, understand that it doesn't define your capacity. Measurements are great indicators of where you are today but horrible indicators for where you will be tomorrow.

Recommended Action: What past measurement have you been allowing to limit your future performance? Prepare yourself for the next measurement whether it's at work, on the field, or just in life, and remind yourself that regardless, it's only a snapshot in time. Fight to grow and expand, but recognize that we all drift. Drift happens. Drift is natural. Acknowledge the drift, and begin to correct it.

Tactic #4: Take Five

If you don't feel peace, stop, and detach from the situation for a moment.

Don't force yourself to operate under the internal pressure.

Yes, many situations will involve pressure, and you need to enter them radiating with contagious confidence, but you don't need to be led by the pressure itself.

Instead, you can learn to be led by peace. This peace will often be felt like a state of clarity and focus, and it will take you far if you allow it. In flight school, we would constantly get screamed at as we were trying to fly. It was like boot camp in the sky:

Oh, my God. Here we go again! Wow, you suck. I can't believe you're making this mistake again. Don't you learn anything, Lieutenant Jones? Turn the aircraft around. Give me the controls.

In those moments, when you just want to jump out of the aircraft and get as far away from your instructor pilot as possible, you must shift into an internal peace. You have to block out the jerk who is screaming at you, and focus on flying the aircraft.

The more I was screamed at, the more my hands would shake on the controls. The more my hands would shake, the more the aircraft would . . . shake. It wasn't fun. But I learned something: chaos might surround you, but it doesn't need to live in you.

I had to override these guys with a louder voice. One that said, *Relax. You can do this. Just fly the aircraft. Block him out.* I found that in just five seconds of putting this practice into place, everything changed.

Recommended Action: How can you begin to implement a trigger *response* in your life instead of reacting to situations? Is there a moment or a phrase that triggers your worst self? How can you train yourself to respond differently? In the future, take five seconds, count backward, and detach from the situation to discover what triggered your pressure. Evaluate your response, apply your training, and re-engage.

CHAOS MIGHT SURROUND YOU, BUT IT DOESN'T NEED TO LIVE IN YOU.

Tactic #5: Establish Rhythms for Recovery

Incorporate daily rhythms to reset and recover by blocking your calendar for a thirty-minute reset.

For a while, I had to do this five times a week every day at noon because life really felt overbearing. At first, I ignored the alert on my phone, telling me it was time to pause, but eventually, I realized that it was needed and began to commit it to my recovery time.

Sunday truly became a day of rest. No work, no business, just family and enjoying the world around us. By teaching myself to implement rhythms for recovery and rest, I began to accept that I didn't have to accomplish everything on my to-do list. I trained myself to put away the phone, headphones, and computer—and just rest.

This is an area I can always improve on, but I noticed tremendous growth as I began to intentionally plan recovery into my schedule.

In her book *Strengthening the Soul of Your Leadership,* Ruth Haley Barton emphasizes the importance of rhythms of rest and recovery by saying the following:

We want to run the race we have been given to run to the best of our ability. We want to last for the long haul. There is nothing more crucial to the staying power of the leader than establishing rhythms that keep us replenished—body, mind and soul. There is nothing more crucial than rhythms that can help us make ourselves available to God for the work that only he can do in us—day in and day out.[59]

Recommended Action: Where can you implement a rhythm of rest and recovery in your life? How can you attach it to an existing activity so that it's an easy transition? This is what James Clear calls habit stacking: "One of the best ways to build a new habit is to identify a current habit you already do each day and then stack your new behavior on top."[60] For instance, I create a routine that after brushing my teeth—which is something I do without even thinking about—I will immediately walk over to my study chair, drink a glass of water, and rest to recover from the day.

Tactic #6: Stewardship

We all know what it's like to walk into a room and feel tension and stress. The same thing happens in our homes. I think, as leaders, we must look for ways to design our environments and steward our atmospheres.

When heavy levels of stress and tension would show up in my home—you know what I mean: the screaming kids, the arguments, the dogs barking, past due bills hitting your account, all that fun stuff—I would search for the best way to shift the state of the atmosphere.

---

[59] Ruth H. Barton, and Gary A. Haugen, *Strengthening the Soul of Your Leadership: Seeking God in the Crucible of Ministry* (Downers Grove, IL: InterVarsity Press, 2018).
[60] James Clear, "How to Build New Habits by Taking Advantage of Old Ones," *James Clear*, 4 Feb. 2020, https://jamesclear.com/habit-stacking.

Recognizing that things were going downhill fast, I would play a specific song or playlist that would shift the vibe without people even noticing it. This is why we train. We train for these moments when we are needed most and when the smallest intervention can change everything.

Bethel Music, *Peace Volume II* has been a game-changer. Just saying.

Recommended Action: In what situation can you begin to introduce a new tool or technique? Maybe there is a song you can play, a show you can turn on, or a phrase you can say. For instance, when stress levels rise, play a song that triggers a calm response in your family members.

Tactic #7: Self-Governance

We are supposed to govern our life, emotions, and body. They are ours to manage.

When I realized that, I began to schedule workouts and create new routines to control stress more effectively. Comedy, exercise, and reading a good book were all different tools that I began to implement into my rhythms.

Self-discipline is not the same as imposed discipline. Don't assume you've developed self-discipline just because you used to wear a uniform or a three-piece suit. I know for me, this is something I had to learn. The military said that at 5 a.m., we were working out; at 8 a.m., we'd assemble for first formation. That's not "self" discipline but "others" discipline. Someone else was scheduling your life for you.

Now, you have a choice. How will you govern yourself?

Recommended Action: Where do you need to better govern and manage your life? What's a great cause of stress that just needs some structure or an outlet to express yourself? The gym is often a great start because you can let that stress out on the weights instead of in your home.

MY PLAN OF ATTACK

What are three tactics you'll choose to deploy with your counterattack? Feel free to borrow mine, or create your own.

Brainstorm and choose. Don't overthink this step. Just pick three that stand out the most, and start deploying each consistently.

Tactic #1:
Tactic #2:
Tactic #3:

ALTAR OF IMPACT COUNTERATTACK

Tactic #1: Give Grace

This had to be one of the most significant adjustments we made as a family. Instead of racking up wins and losses against one another, we implemented a trigger phrase that we both agreed carried more weight than any score.

Here it is.

We would say, "Could you just give me grace?"

At that moment, it didn't matter what was wrong or how much someone had messed up. Jess and I both believe in the power of grace, and we gave it. We all make mistakes. We aren't perfect. Marriage is hard. We all say mean things sometimes. But what would happen if we deployed grace?

Instead of making excuses for why I forgot to put the groceries away or justifying why I forgot to pay a bill, I said, "Look, I'm sorry. Could you give me grace?

That started a revolution! Not only did it help release the feeling of tension, but it also created a deeper connection in our relationship. We both needed grace, so the more it was asked for, the more it was given. It's like no matter what happened, we would drop it and just accept that we all make mistakes, no further explanation needed.

Something powerful happens to a marriage in those moments.

Recommended Action: Where can you deploy grace today? Find one area of your life—maybe either with your kids or spouse—and begin to teach them the power of grace by giving it when they need it most. Next time your kid colors on the wall, give grace. Next time your teenager hits your car with a lacrosse ball, give grace. Next time your spouse totally blows it, give grace.

Tactic #2: Transition With Intention

Oh, boy. I'm excited to share this one with you.

A few years ago, I was meeting with a performance coach, and I explained to him that my wife said I was never present. I told him that she thought I wasn't listening, but I was. I didn't have work on my mind. I was there with her. I said that when I got home from work, I would turn my brain off and be with her fully.

He said, "Wait, you turn your brain off?"

"Yep!" I replied.

"Well, that's why she says you're not present. Your brain is off."

He taught me that I didn't need to turn my brain off, but I could transition my brain, mind, and energy into the new role that I was stepping into. So instead of turning my mind off when I got home, I learned to transition my mind into husband and father mode.

These effective transitions can be attached to a daily trigger that reminds you to shift your focus or intention. For me, when I touch the doorknob to my house, I transition my mind, and I remind myself, *Right now is the time to bring my best self as a father and husband.* Then I walk in, and it's go time.

Recommended Action: So many of us want to rest or take a break the second we walk through the door after a long day of work, but the truth is we can't coast. We need to transition. How can you transition your mind to fully focus on being a present parent and spouse? What consistent action in your day can you use to trigger the transition? Pick a trigger, and begin to use it. Remember that there is power in your presence.

Tactic #3:. Deploy Appreciation

Let your spouse know they are seen and appreciated, but do this in the way that matters to them.

Show appreciation in the way that they need it—not in the way that's easiest for you.

If you haven't read the book *The 5 Love Languages*, this is a must-read. The author, Gary Chapman, explains that people feel loved and show love in different ways. He calls them love languages.[61] They include the following:

1) Words of Affirmation
2) Quality Time
3) Receiving Gifts
4) Acts of Service
5) Physical Touch

By default, we all communicate that we love someone by our preferred language—the way we feel loved by others—but it might not speak to the person we love the same way. The more we understand

---

61 Gary D. Chapman, *The 5 Love Languages* (Chicago, IL: Northfield Publishing, 2014).

about ourselves and those we love, the more likely we are to feel and give love in meaningful ways.

For instance, my wife's love language is acts of service. This means if I want to show her that I love and appreciate her, I'll sweep the house, clean the dishes, and take out the trash. My love language is words of affirmation. This means if she wants to tell me that she loves and appreciates me, she will say it. They are not the same. My job is to communicate to her through acts of service; her job is to communicate through words of affirmation. Get it?

Telling her how much she matters, thanking her often, and showing physical affection randomly do communicate love. But helping with dishes without being asked or scratching her back at night—those she *feels*. I'm speaking her language. All of these moments add up to her feeling loved and our family being unified.

Recommended Action: What is your preferred love language, and what is your spouse's? What are your kids' love languages? Once you determine these, begin to take the necessary steps to communicate to them they are appreciated and loved in the ways that matter most to them.

Tactic #4: Schedule Reminders

A huge thing that helped me get into the motion of reaching out to my wife and maybe surprising her with a text was by scheduling reminders in my phone.

No joke.

I know it sounds pathetic, but I'm tunnel-visioned.

Once my head is down, and I'm working on something, I'm all in, and it takes an act of God to pull me away from it. Or . . . a notification on my phone.

That's why, for a while, in order to build the muscle of attentiveness, I would just have an alert on my phone set for each day to send a text to Jess and ask how her day was. Reaching out to her sounds simple, but it goes a long way. Now, I don't have to use these reminders. I just remember and have her on my mind. (Mind blown, right?)

Recommended Action: How can you schedule reminders to guide your actions? These could be reminders to send a text or give a call. This might be daily, weekly, or monthly. Just find out what works, and do it. As high-performance leaders, we tend to put the blinders on, and we need to set up triggers to bring our awareness back to our family.

Tactic #5:. Define Your Home

When something has a name, we tend to care for it with more intentionality. That's why when parents take their kids to a pet store just to "see" the animals, they say, "Don't name that dog, or you'll want to keep it." Something happens in our brain—an emotional investment takes place—when we assign a name to something we care about.

In the military, we named our squad, our barracks, and our parade field, so why wouldn't we name our home? We named our home The Fourtress. It's not just the place where the *four* of us live. It's also the location from which we operate and move into mission—a mission to move mountains and make the world a better place. A mission to invite others into our life and to encourage people around us anywhere we go.

It's simple, but it makes a difference.

Recommended Action: Get your family together, and name your home. Ask each person what they would name it. It'll give you a glimpse into what "home" means to them. Then, together, come up with a name everyone can agree on.

Tactic #6: Implement Date Days

We implemented date days on a monthly basis, and it changed the game!

For over a year, we didn't go on one date by ourselves. Anytime we went out to eat, a kid was with us. Make no mistake about it—this is not a date. It's dinner, and your spouse needs one-on-one time with you.

I know it might be expensive; budget appropriately. Your marriage matters, right?

One day, we decided if our girls were at daycare, we should use that opportunity to go on a date day. Now we schedule one each month, and it is seriously one of the days we look forward to more than anything else.

While other people are at work, we are using our paid time off, and our kids are in daycare.

By the way, I am a visionary—not a logistician. This means I HATE planning events. However, my wife LOVES planning events. In the past, I thought in order to surprise her with a date, I had to plan it. What I found was that I just needed to let her know a date and maybe a theme, and then she would jump onto her phone and start planning. We leveraged each other's strengths.

It didn't end there. I also started to schedule days with my daughters. Addy Daddy Days and Aspen Daddy Days (sorry, this one doesn't rhyme) are the best. Again, the same thing applies. I put the date in my calendar, and then Jess helps me plan it. These don't need to be long events. Daddy-daughter dates usually last just two to three hours, but they make a huge difference.

Recommended Action: What would your marriage look like if you went on a date every month for a year? What would your relationship with your kids look like if you had one event a month with each one of them over the course of a year? Coordinate with your spouse to get a date on the calendar. And then, here's the secret: before one date is over, make sure the next one is already on the schedule.

MY PLAN OF ATTACK

What are three tactics you'll choose to deploy with your counterattack? Feel free to borrow mine, or create your own.

Tactic #1:
Tactic #2:
Tactic #3:

CYCLE OF COMPARISON COUNTERATTACK

Tactic #1: Unification

Everyone in our home knows who we are and what we bring to the table. We know we are not identical, but we are united. Now, I know that's easy to say with a toddler and infant, but trust me, we won't let this one slip. Plus, the baby is already picking up on what we are teaching.

Our goal is not uniformity but unity. Learn how to position your family to leverage each other's strengths. Think to yourself how you operate as a family where everyone's function matters. I can't help but think about the movie *The Incredibles*—each family member has superpowers, and they must work together to fight evil.[62]

My daughters each have three core attributes to who they are. For example, my firstborn is joyful, compassionate, and fierce. This is core to understanding who she is. The moment someone is hurt, her compassion is activated. She doesn't have to force it; it's just who she is. Her joy fills the room with laughter and silliness. Her fierceness is

---

62 Brad Bird, *The Incredibles* (Nov. 5, 2004; Burbank, CA: Walt Disney Studios and Pixar Studios).

activated to push her through different challenges, and yes . . . to get an extra piece of candy.

My younger daughter is bold, strong, and courageous. She isn't even one year old yet, and I can see it. I hear her loud, powerful, bold war cry. I can see her hulk-like strength. I can see her courage when climbing obstacles around the house.

It's my job to see who they are and then say it to them. This is how they learn how we complement one another instead of compete with one another.

Recommended Action: Begin to look at your family as a high-performing team that you're the head coach for. Search for their strengths, and align everyone accordingly. If you listen to my podcast at adamfjones.com or grab some of my free resources on the site, you'll hear a lot more about this tactic and how you can maximize the strengths of your home team.

Tactic #2: Change the Volume

When pilots set up their systems and radio in a cockpit, they learn that some radios need to be louder than others. Most of the time, we would have five different sources that could speak to us while we were on a mission. Which one should be the loudest? If both speak at the same time (which happens all the time, by the way), which one do I need to hear the most?

Applying this to my life, I began to become more disciplined and vigilant with whom I allowed to influence my thoughts and how I compared myself to others. There were some amazing influencers and leaders that I would listen to on YouTube or a podcast that would cause me to enter a state of hurry. Whenever I listened to them, I felt behind and overwhelmed.

My wife could feel it.

Knowing this, I turned the volume of their voices down, and I began to listen to what caused me to be a more pleasant human being. (I know—who would have thought, right?) I turned down the volume of hustle and grind and raised the volume for those who spoke about the power of presence.

Most importantly, God's voice in my heart has become the loudest voice. If someone insinuates that I'm not good enough, or they are "giving me a shot," in the past, I would have felt my confidence drop. But now, I immediately hear the voice in my heart saying, *They just don't see what I see yet.*

Recommended Action: What sources in your life need to have the volume raised, and which sources need the volume to be brought down? What sources need to be shut off? The voices we allow to speak into our life determine the direction of our life. Identify those sources and adjust the volume accordingly.

Tactic #3: Establish Boundaries

Limit your time on social media.

This one is obvious, but are you doing it?

I love to leverage social media to help others and connect with new people, but it doesn't take a lot for me to start seeing someone else's success and then think, *I'm better than them. That's not fair.*

I'm not proud to share that. It's such a cowardly and selfish thought, but regardless, it happened, and we aren't our thoughts. Thoughts just appear. Aren't we all made by the same God, by the same Father? Then, why am I trash-talking someone else's success? It just doesn't make sense.

In 2022, I asked God to help me with one thing. I asked Him to help me have His heart for His people. It's a continual process, but I have definitely seen improvement. Most of the time, when I see someone else crushing it, instead of feeling jealous about their success, I just feel so proud to see them reaching the next level. (Most of the time . . . again, I'm a work in progress)

Recommended Action: How much more would people want to join forces with you if you actually applauded their success and meant it? Ask God for His heart for His people, and then take the next step and let others know how proud you are of their progression.

Tactic #4: Deploy Gratitude

How many times do we have to hear that we should practice gratitude before we actually do it?

I don't know about you, but it's so easy to see someone else's success and only think about my failure. It's like I'm wired for jealousy. Or was I programmed with it?

Before the release of Gary Vaynerchuk's book *Twelve and a Half*, he reminded the world about the importance of gratitude with the following statement:

> *I truly believe that gratitude is one of the most underrated traits. Many of you may also remember "400 Trillion to One." For those of you who didn't know, those are the actual odds of you becoming a human being. . . . If that doesn't make you feel grateful, I don't know what will.*[63]

I mean, think about that.

You were created. There is no one else like you.

---

[63] Gary Vaynerchuk, "Road to Twelve and a Half: Gratitude," *Gary Vaynerchuk*, 20 Sept. 2021, https://garyvaynerchuk.com/road-to-twelve-and-a-half-gratitude/.

Recommended Action: Implement a practice of gratitude, and you'll begin to see what you have instead of what is missing. Hunt for the good. Train your mind to see the opportunities and blessings in front of you.

MY PLAN OF ATTACK
What are three tactics you'll choose to deploy with your counterattack? Feel free to borrow mine, or create your own.

Tactic #1:

Tactic #2:

Tactic #3:

TRAP OF TITLE COUNTERATTACK
Tactic #1: Operational Alignment

Who we are determines what we are meant to do. This means we still take action, but we recognize that our performance does not determine our identity.

As a speaker, it's easy to get caught up in that title. But what happens if I don't have other stages to speak on? What happens when life changes, and I go through more transitions? Here's what I've found: instead of focusing on the profession, go deeper into the root element of that activity. For instance, I've come to believe that I'm a voice and a sound. I can always be a voice and a sound. I'm not limited by someone else's perspective or a past position. See, a sound doesn't put me in a box of restrictions that requires a certain position or title. A sound carries with me everywhere I go. Why? Because it's who I am.

Tim Grover is recognized as the trainer of the most elite, iconic athletes in the world, including the late Kobe Bryant, Michael Jordan, and Dwayne Wade. Tim says, "In order to have what you really want, you must first be who you really are."[64]

That's one of the greatest shifts I made in my life. I know who I am. I know what that means. And when I show up, I know what other people should expect from me. I operate out of alignment, not ambition.

Recommended Action: What level of confidence would you operate with if you knew exactly who you are? Go deeper with this and begin to look for signs. Pray and study the patterns in your life to discover who you are. What results arrive when you show up?

Tactic #2: Leverage Your Labels

Understanding that a title is meant for leverage—not limits—helped me expand my mind to see what was possible for my life after the uniform. Titles are important. Hierarchy is needed, but I had to understand that my title was something to be leveraged to help others, not limit myself. As a former service member, executive, administrator, or first responder, you can use this experience to serve others, but first, you must learn to connect with them.

I remember thinking that I didn't want to only say I was a Black Hawk pilot because I was more than that. I'm also a father, a husband, an entrepreneur, and a coach. We can't be limited by one title. You are much more than a veteran, soldier, officer, executive, coach, administrator, or whatever else comes to mind.

Recommended Action: How would you operate if you began to see your titles as leverage, not limits? Can you begin to use your title to serve other people? Take a moment to slow down and think about how you can use your title to lift other people up.

---

[64] Tim S. Grover and Shari Lesser Wenk, *Relentless: From Good to Great to Unstoppable* (New York, NY: Scribner, 2014).

Tactic #3: Think Like an Ambassador

You might not feel like you have the appropriate title, but are you being sent by someone or something? Are you representing your family or another organization? Someone is most likely vouching for you and preparing the way for you. It's possible that this is all you need. In the Army, if a captain worked as the assistant for the general, then when they were sent on behalf of the general, that general's rank is what got them in the door. You might not have the right title, but if God is opening the doors, and you have solutions, you don't really need one.

Ambassadors are sent to represent the affairs of a nation. When I move through life, I have a "Sent Mentality." I have a belief that I am positioned for purpose and that I am sent to a particular location for a reason. This is that mission mindset that causes you to see life with intentionality and anticipation. It's a mindset that guides the way you see life and that trains you to look for the opportunities hidden in the obstacles.

Additionally, one thing I teach organizations that I work with when I'm developing their leaders is that each is an ambassador of all the different aspects of their life. They are an ambassador for their family name, they are an ambassador for their school, and they are an ambassador for their team. Amazing things happen when we think bigger than ourselves.

Recommended Action: Train yourself to operate with solutions, not qualifications. You might have a qualification, but without an answer to someone's question, it's not helpful to them. Instead of focusing on racking up qualifications, focus on delivering solutions that solve problems. The doors will open for that.

Tactic #4: Close the Gap

There is probably a major relatability gap between the life you've lived and the lives of the people you lead. If you used to be a soldier, you might have no idea how to connect with civilians because your path has been so different. It's hard to find common ground. They might try to understand things about your life at the surface level, but you need to close the gap.

CBS even produced a reality show called *Undercover Boss*, on which high-level "executives [went] undercover to examine the inner workings of their company." The whole purpose of the show was to allow the leader of the company or organization to see what was happening on lower levels. Whether workers were rewarded for their hard work or given additional training or support, the end result was a closing of the gap between those with the greatest authority and those with the least.

As high-performing leaders, I recommend that we start doing our part by helping others see us for more than what we do or represent. Connect with people based on what they want to chat about and what matters most to them. I know this sounds challenging, and it is. But that's leadership. If we want to broaden our influence, then we have to first see ourselves as more than what we've been, and we have to see others as more than what we've seen them in the past.

We are not opposing forces. We are on the same team. Some of us are used to suffering physical hardship. Others of us have worked excruciatingly long hours to get where we are. Still, others have laid down our lives to serve. Help the people you lead develop in these areas as well.

Recommended Action: Look for people whom you are leading or connecting to, and see how you can close the gap. Leaders go first. You don't need to wait for them. Just take the first step, and attempt to close the gap. Even as a parent, lean down, and approach your grumpy toddler or your withdrawn teenager with understanding. Only then will they allow you to teach them about the situation.

Tactic #5: Train for Tomorrow

On my podcast, I talk about the four actions you can take when life puts you in what I call a *Holding Pattern*. You're not moving forward or making any discernible progress. A lot of people are frustrated by their lack of title because they feel they are waiting until the next opportunity comes.

I wonder if, instead of only waiting, we could train on the fundamentals. This is what I learned to do as a pilot, and it's what I learned to do as a speaker. As a pilot, if we were placed in a holding pattern, it was for a good reason. Sometimes, it was to train. Other times, it was because we were being set up for an approach, and we needed to wait for other aircraft to land. Either way, there is a purpose to the holding pattern in the air and in our lives.

When I didn't have a full calendar as a speaker, I used that time to hone my craft—to prepare and train on the basics: how to start a keynote or how to connect with my audience. I would study the great speakers and see how they kept their messages simple but inspiring. I might not have had the position or title that I wanted, but I had the same opportunity you have today: the opportunity to train. Train in your time of waiting, and stay ready for the next opportunity to appear.

It's not as far as you think.

Recommended Action: If you are stuck in a holding pattern right now, determine if this is a time to train on the fundamentals. If you are looking to progress into a new career, train for it. Start to add the skills you need to move into the position you want.

MY PLAN OF ATTACK

What are three tactics you'll choose to deploy with your counterattack? Feel free to use mine, or create your own.

Tactic #1:

Tactic #2:

Tactic #3:

CHAPTER 21
BLUE SKY

As we start our last chapter, it all comes down to our choosing what is right for our lives based on the results we want. Input leads to output. If we're not getting the results we want in a reasonable amount of time, then we need to ask:

1) What do we need to change about the way we are living?
2) What do we need to change about our environment?
3) What do we need to change about the way we steward ourselves?

That is—I hope—what this book, *Weapons of Mass Deception,* has been doing for you because that's what it's been designed to help you do: *Define* a weapon that you most likely didn't know existed but that you experience every day of your life. *Detect* how that weapon has been targeting your heart, home, and headquarters. *Dismantle* the weapon by disrupting the complex patterns concealing its presence. *Deploy* an aggressive counterattack to recover what was lost and prevent future damage. *Equip* you with the language to describe and destroy what's been affecting you the most. *Break* complex relational dynamics down into manageable components that you can actually process and progress beyond.

THE BLUE SKY LEADERSHIP STRATEGY

As I briefly mentioned, much of what I have shared with you throughout this book stems from an extensive leadership development strategy that I've built by working with top-tier leaders. This strategy has been used to train corporate executives, military leaders, professional and collegiate athletes, and many other high-performance teams. The key to the strategy is that before we add, we must subtract. Most of this book was focused on just that: subtraction.

Even though we haven't dived into the details, I think it's important that you see the bigger picture. The model listed below depicts the intersections between what I call the three specializations: command presence, situational awareness, and mission readiness. Leaders who have developed their *Command Presence* are influential and attractive. People want to follow those leaders because they know who they are, what they are meant to do, and how they can draw out the best in others. Leaders who have developed their *Situational Awareness* are effective and able to see more and before other people. They are trained to maximize their resources and align others to operate with intentionality. Leaders who have developed their *Mission Readiness* are resilient and have prepared their team members for promotion. They have built the disciplines and rhythms needed to operate at higher levels.

At the intersection of these three specializations, we see the formation of the transformational leader—you.

Through each page, you've been trained with components from the three specializations to help you not only experience transformation for yourself but extend it into your home and community. A transformation is a thorough change in form or appearance. Have you begun to see yourself and the world around you in a new way? Then it's working. You have been experiencing transformation, and you can extend it to others.

Believe it or not, we are just getting started. Now that you've removed the extra weight and reduced your loadout, you'll be able to strategically add in tactics and components from the three specializations as your journey continues. When we are properly trained in each of these specializations, we will operate with consistent levels of confidence, clarity, and conviction.

I remember a moment when I was walking out to an aircraft on a beautiful Monday morning, and I looked over to my instructor pilot. He smiled and said, "Looks like it's clear, blue, and twenty-two today."

I had never heard that phrase before, so I asked him to clarify.

He said, "Blue sky. Clear with twenty-two miles of visibility. Look, look up there, man. There's no clouds. There's no weather. You can see as far to the horizon as your eyes will let you. It's blue sky."

There was something about that phrase that describes what life looks like without these weapons in your path. Today, that's the life I live. *Blue Sky.*

Yes, life is still hard.

Yes, marriage and parenting take a lot of work.

Yes, I have to constantly discipline myself to stay available to the people who need me most.

But . . . I'm living a blue sky life.

I'm enjoying the journey. I'm progressing toward my destiny, and I'm free from any guilt and shame of the past. When a weapon comes in my crosshairs, it's defeated because I won't stand to see my family caught up in that mess again. I'm free.

I hope with each day you move closer to a blue sky reality. I pray you are no longer maxed out, weighed down, stressed, and drifting. I hope you are beginning to experience the joy and freedom of *Blue Sky*. That's what you've been working to create: a Blue Sky life for you and those you love. You are becoming a transformational leader—a blue sky leader—who helps others experience clarity and peace as they navigate life's most challenging obstacles.

Using this strategy, we not only detect and defeat the weapons of mass deception, but we begin to assemble *Weapons of Mass Transformation*. (That's right; get ready for a sequel!)

IF FREEDOM IS WORTH FIGHTING FOR . . .
AND IF FREEDOM IS WORTH DYING FOR . . .
THEN FREEDOM IS WORTH LIVING FOR.

The greatest leaders are not leaders who have more than you. They are leaders who have become effective at making sure that they choose less. They give themselves fully to their family, to a business, or to a cause, and they keep it simple and clear. They filter the distractions and focus on what matters most. They are soaring in blue sky. They are not overwhelmed. They are enjoying the flight because they believe in what they are fighting for.

For me, the ultimate fight is the fight for freedom.

If freedom is worth fighting for . . .

And if freedom is worth dying for . . .
Then freedom is worth living for.

OPERATION RESTORATION

Now that you've completed this book, you can feel confidence and conviction that your next days will be your best days. However, I have one final secret to share with anyone who has read this far. We have viewed the weapons of mass deception exclusively as if they are offensive weapons—as if their purpose is to gain territory for darkness.

There is another way we can look at them. Are you ready for the final secret?

What if you have not been attacked, but you are the attack?

What if each weapon is simply a defensive measure to slow down the advancement of the light living within you?

What if—by disrupting a kill chain and dismantling a weapon of mass deception—you are defeating the desperate defenses of darkness?

If this is true, what does it say about you? It says you are valuable. You are powerful. You are stronger than you've ever imagined. You are a source of freedom and inspiration for those around you. You are a leader with influence.

Considering that, what does it say about you NOW that you've been equipped to detect and defeat these weapons?

We cannot give what we do not have. We cannot transform the world around us until we experience transformation within us. Therefore, if you are growing from a maxed-out leader to a transformational leader, and if you have become a chain breaker, then you will help others break free. You are an instrument of hope sent out to bring transformation to a hurting world.

YOU ARE AN INSTRUMENT OF HOPE SENT OUT TO BRING TRANSFORMATION TO A HURTING WORLD.

What if all it takes for the rest of the world to enter into the greatest stage of peace, purpose, power, freedom, love, strength, and joy is simply to defeat the weapons? To break through the defenses of darkness. For me, that was the case. You know I was suffocating in a storm, wandering in the wilderness. unable to see a way out, and going to lose it all. The weapons were the reason. They were deterring, delaying, dissuading, and destroying not only my heart but my home and many others through my influence. Lots of other people are in that situation.

The fight doesn't end with this book. Now that you've been equipped, you'll notice in conversations with friends and family members that these weapons are present in their lives as well. It happens all the time. I'll be chatting with a new client, my wife, or a friend, and they'll be sharing about a man who feels like he isn't good enough or a woman who relies on her title to inform her identity, and each time I say, "You know what? That's one of the weapons!"

They'll often respond, "You're totally right!"

At that point, I can offer a new tactic or strategy that could help them get free, and that person and I have engaged in Operation Restoration.

You will encounter these weapons again along your path. Before long, you'll notice a weapon or two appearing when you thought you had defeated them. This is normal. Defeating these weapons is an ongoing practice, but you know the process: define, detect, dismantle, and deploy.

You can do this.

Not only for you but for others.

I want to challenge you: get this message out there to just one more person.

Who needs to know there is power in their presence and that their present location does not dictate their future destiny?

Would you share this with them? I can't do this on my own because there are people only you can reach. I wrote the book, but I'm looking for messengers and leaders to get this message of freedom and transformation into homes all across the globe.

Why?

Because I believe the family unit is the most valuable resource in the world. It is irreplaceable. When families are unified and *restored,* we will see our neighborhoods, communities, workplaces, towns, cities, states, and nations transformed. Operation Restoration is part of that effort.

THERE IS POWER IN YOUR PRESENCE.

Move forward, advance with confidence, and take back any ground that has been stolen from you. Fight for your freedom. Recover all that has been lost. These weapons steal peace, purpose, and power, and you know what to do. Remember the origins of the weapon, acknowledge your drift, trust your instruments, use the key indicators to detect the weapons, map out their kill chains, train yourself to discern deception from truth, and press forward with power to the greatest stage of your life.

There is power in your presence.

You were only attracting the attention of the weapons of mass deception because you are the greatest threat to the advancement of a spirit of fear. You are not being attacked. The weapons are shielding themselves against you. You aren't encountering an aggressive assault but a desperate defense. You may not always see it, but there is something very good inside of you, and each day it's fighting to be released.

It's been an honor to write this book and take this journey with you.

Now use it on the next leg of your journey.

And remember this: whether you are at the top of a peak or the bottom of a pit—*Continue Mission.*

PHASE 4 SUMMARY

KEY TERMS
- Counterattack—an attack made in response to one by an enemy or opponent.
- Tactic—an action or strategy carefully planned to achieve a specific end.

KEY CONSIDERATIONS
- Counterattacks for the Pressure of Performance
    1) Silence
    2) Seek to Understand
    3) Strategic Awareness
    4) Take Five
    5) Establish Rhythms for Recovery
    6) Stewardship
    7) Self-Governance
- Counterattacks for the Altar of Impact
    1) Give Grace
    2) Transition With Intention
    3) Deploy Appreciation
    4) Schedule Reminders
    5) Define Your Home
    6) Implement Date Days
- Counterattacks for the Cycle of Comparison
    1) Unification
    2) Change the Volume

    3) Establish Boundaries
    4) Deploy Gratitude
> Counterattacks for the Trap of Title
    1) Operational Alignment
    2) Leverage Your Labels
    3) Think Like an Ambassador
    4) Close the Gap
    5) Train for Tomorrow

SUMMARY

You carry a light that infiltrates the darkness. The light always wins. Weapons of mass deception are fragile and easily defeated once they are detected. Use the counterattacks to take back the ground that has been stolen from you. Your family will see a change in you, but none of this happens overnight. The process of recovering lost ground will take weeks, months, and even years, but you can do this. Give yourself, your family, and your friends grace during this time. You will stumble on your journey, but through a consistent application of the tactics provided, you will experience a Blue Sky life. This is possibly the most important fight of your life. Freedom is worth it.

NEXT STEPS

Consider leaving a review on Amazon. Share this book with one other person. Follow Adam on social media. Go to adamfjones.com to book a training or event for your company.

ABOUT THE AUTHOR

Adam F. Jones is a transformational speaker, leadership consultant, and the founder of Kingdom Operatives—a leadership development company that equips leaders to build transformational teams using his Blue Sky Leadership Strategy. Best-known for his real and raw thought leadership on topics such as compassionate candor and mission mindset, Adam's training continues to help executives, collegiate teams, and military leaders activate the power in their presence.

Adam was awarded the Army Commendation Medal for his achievements with team leadership as a former U.S. Army Captain, Company Commander, and UH-60 Black Hawk helicopter pilot.

Despite achieving his childhood dream of becoming a Black Hawk pilot, Adam eventually found himself feeling frustrated, lost, and empty. It was in that moment that he began to detect and defeat the Weapons of Mass Deception that were hidden in his own heart. Since winning the war for his home, he has committed himself to bringing this message of freedom to high-capacity leaders around the world.

He lives in Pittsburgh, Pennsylvania, with his wife, Jessica, and their daughters, Adalynne and Aspen.

Visit AdamFJones.com for more tools and resources to help build your team.

AdamFJones.com

Facebook, Instagram, Twitter, and Linked-In @LeadWithAdam

ACKNOWLEDGMENTS

I'm standing on the shoulders of giants. Many people have shaped me into becoming the leader that I am today. If I wrote of them all, it would fill a book. I would like to specifically acknowledge anyone who helped me develop this book—whether through a conversation, a breakthrough, or the expansion of an idea. Writing a book is tough work. There were many times when I wanted to quit, but I felt a responsibility to press on. Most days, I had to find a way to write this in the early mornings—3 to 5 a.m.—before the girls woke up and the late nights—10 p.m. to midnight—when everyone was asleep. It took everything I had, but you, my fellow reader, were worth it. These are some people who made it all happen:

I have to start by thanking the Lord. Without Him, this book would have never been written, and my marriage wouldn't have made it. My family is restored because of Him. He did things I could never explain. He transformed my heart. This book, though limited by me, was inspired by Him.

Jessica, you are such a powerful woman. You make me better every day. You are the true warrior-princess. You are an inspiration. I see you for who you are, and I love it. The more I tell the story of this time in our life, the more I realize that the greatest gift . . . has been you. Thank you for staying strong and patient and for trusting that the change was happening. You have helped me develop these concepts in our daily conversations, and I've never been happier to have you on my side.

Adalynne, thank you for helping me grow into the father I needed to be. You have always been so loving. Remember: you are joyful, compassionate, and fierce. Thank you for bringing me home. You did more than you could ever imagine. Moments with you kept me fighting to find peace and joy. I found it. I can't wait for you to see who you are meant to be.

Aspen, thank you for being hilarious and for being an easy baby. I'm honored to be your father. Since you're only eleven months old, I don't have much to go off of right now, but thank you for coming into our life. You have made our home even more special. Laughter and joy fill our home, and you are part of that. Remember: you are bold, strong, and courageous. I can't wait for you to see who you are meant to be.

***

To everyone else who inspired the creation of this book through the long conversations with leaders in my life, mentors, and family. You had such a major role in my transformation. You didn't just save me. You saved my family and many people whom this message will reach. Never doubt: there is power in your presence.

Thanks to everyone on the Four Rivers Media team who helped me get this message into production. Special thanks to Andy, the perfect thoughtful editor to complement such an intense message; Debbie, my amazing publishing manager, keeping us on track with all the intricacies of this effort; John, the fast-moving coordination machine who taught me to level up my mindset; Martijn, the man who saw the heart behind my message; and Nicky, for getting this book in front of the team and leading me to find peace when it hurt the most.

Thanks to my ministry family who brought ridiculous levels of transformation into my life. Special thanks to Dr. Israel and Rebecca, one of the greatest blessings in my life who brought these breakthroughs into reality; David and Margo, the Spirit-led catalysts who led us to see the opportunities in the adversity of the weapons; and Richard and Chasity, the family who keeps believing and who encouraged me when I felt destroyed by the pressure of performance.

Thanks to my father and mother who have always been there. Can you believe your kid wrote a book? Mom, I've always enjoyed our talks. You taught me how to connect with myself and with others. That was critical for this book. You always knew I was going to sell something, and now we know what it is—my words. Dad, you taught me patience and how to work persistently with a smile on my face. That trait helped me stay consistent when I didn't want to keep writing.

Thanks to Andy and Nancy, my amazing in-laws, who have been there when I needed them the most. Thank you for loving and spoiling my girls, all three of them. Our conversations helped me develop these concepts with deeper clarity and understanding.

Thanks to my Nana, who taught me to love and accept people for who they are. Unfortunately, you passed two months before this book was published, but without knowing it, you were critical to the development of my transformation and this message. Conversations with you changed my life.

To the people who will read this book. Writing a book about the story of your life and the depths of your pain isn't really that fun. I know it sounds great to say you wrote a book. What a cool accomplishment, right? Well, this book basically exposed all the pain of my past, but it's brought me to find the potential in my future. This book requires me to talk about my failures on a daily basis, but YOU were worth it. I wrote this book for you—that one person who is ready to find freedom and who knows the best days are not the last days.

To everyone who supports and works with Kingdom Operatives. I'm honored to serve you. Thank you for allowing me to be a voice in your life. Thank you to Lindsay for joining with me to launch the company and serve in a labor of love for the betterment of leaders around North America. Our conversations brought freedom to my heart. To my clients and team members both now and in the future, I hope this encourages you. Remember: Fear falls when we focus on others. Fear loses its power when you shift your focus. You have been sent for purpose and deployed for destiny. Lead with love and Continue Mission.

Next, to all those who have also played a key role in the development of the breakthroughs in this book, even if you didn't know it: Dan, Marc, Dave, Greg, Roy, Rob, Dubb, Ryan, John Mark, Iris, Joshua, Zack, and Lauren.

Finally, to the *Messengers*, those who believed in the message and contributed their time and resources to get it out to readers. Thank you. We all owe you tremendous gratitude. You made this message available. I know you've heard this before, but I really have something against independence. "Self-made" just doesn't feel right to me. I don't think we can be truly great at anything ourselves. We need each other. So thank you for coming together and contributing to get this information packaged and delivered to the reader—the right way.

There are more Messengers every month, but listed below are a few that I can acknowledge today. If you would like to join them, email us at admin@adamfjones.com, asking to set up a meeting or a contribution. You can purchase book bundles, contribute monthly, or give one-time gifts to help us get this message in the hands of more leaders. The more Messengers we have, the more books we can produce, and the more transformation we will see.

To the Messengers: Jessica, Greg and Susan, Richard and Chasity, Dale, Dan, Mom and Dad, Andrew, Andrey, Lyndsie and JT, Carolyn, Kelly, Josh, Marc, Andy, and DJ.

CPSIA information can be obtained
at www.ICGtesting.com
Printed in the USA
BVHW050119200223
658797BV00012B/2433